D1087065

The Orchards Poetry Journal

Summer Issue 2023

ISBN: 978-1-63980-420-7

Karen Kelsay, Editor-in-Chief
Jenna V. Wray, Co-Editor
Delisa Hargrove, Assistant Editor
Shay Culligan, Cover Design

For submissions, visit our website at
orchardspoetry.com

Inspired by the small plot of apple trees near Cambridge, England, where writers have gathered for years with their books and pens, we welcome you to pull up a chair and enjoy poetry in the orchard.

The Grantchester Award Winners

First Place $50.00

1. Megan Wildhood, "Evaporation" (63)

Second Place $30.00

2. Ruth Towne, "So the Sadness Could Not Hurt" (171)

Pushcart Nominations

1. Samuel Samba, "Hardened in no small way" (70)

2. Elinor Ann Walker, "Highway 64, Tennessee" (110)

3. Grace Martin, "Tracking the Source, Losing the Trail" (121)

Summer 2023

Contents

Summer 2023

Summer 2023

Summer 2023

Summer 2023

Summer 2023

Summer 2023

Featured Poet

REBECCA BROCK

First-Place Winner of the 2022 Women's Contest

How would you describe your poetic style?

My poems concern themselves with the everyday, the domestic—
my lived experience, our vulnerability. My style tends toward small
narratives, tangible imagery, and direct language. I'm not trying to
keep anyone out. I love Edna O'Brien's quote from a *Paris Review*
interview. She talked about the "obsession" of writing, how, "from
the beginning" it "derives from an intensity of feeling which normal
life cannot accommodate." I think, for me, that's it exactly.

Who are the poets who inspire you?

Some writers show us how. I remember the first time I read Ellen
Bass's poem "Indigo"—the want in it, the revelation, and the rush.
Reading Lucille Clifton's "Lazarus"—the first day—where Lazarus
is "swiveling in the light"—that is a poem, a moment in the poem,
that undoes me every time I read it. I lean toward the feminine:
Louise Glück, Marie Howe, Sharon Olds; and contemporary poets:
Remica Bingham-Risher, Ada Limón, Jane Hirshfield, Kelly Russel
Agodon, Maggie Smith, Ocean Vuong, Hanif Willis-Abudurraqib.
I read a lot of literary magazines, and I read for *SWWIM*—I love the
gasp and the knowing when a poet has succeeded with voice, with
aim, content, image.

*As the winner of the Women's Poetry Contest (Kelsay Books), Muriel
Craft Bailey Memorial Poetry Contest (The Comstock Review), and
two Editor's Choice Awards (Sheila-Na-Gig Online), you are clearly
no stranger to contests. How do you decide which poems to submit?*

I've been very lucky. I do my homework, researching past winners,
what the publisher has published, and the final judges. The Women's
Poetry Contest and the Muriel Craft Bailey Contest were judged by
Katie Manning and Ellen Bass, respectively. Both have inspired me
with their own work. I chose poems I thought they might like, if my
poems were lucky enough to reach them in the final rounds.

Summer 2023

In 2022, Kelsay Books published your chapbook Each Bearing Out. *For poets who have individual poems published but never put together a chapbook, what would you tell them about the process?*

I was given the option of an extended leave from my job as a flight attendant in the early part of Covid. I told myself, if I took it, that I would piece together a chapbook. Calling it a chapbook focused my theme and scope—and that helped me get my mind around the idea. I wasn't trying to write a book . . . I was only working on a chapbook.

I read a lot of chapbooks. And I looked up deadlines and used them as goalposts. I found poets whose work I admired, in journals I liked, and ordered their books. Submitting my poems individually provided a sort of scaffolding; I knew certain poems had resonance and strength. As for what to include and how to arrange, I relied mostly on instinct. I read them out loud, a lot, and paid particular attention to what would be the first and last poem. I even printed them out, sorted, arranged, and rearranged them physically, by hand, all down the hallway in my basement.

Why did you choose Kelsay Books as your first publisher?

Kelsay Books was recommended to me by several people—editors and writers alike. I already owned books published by Kelsay authors, so I knew they produced beautiful books. When I submitted to Kelsay, I heard back very soon, and the entire process was clear and very straightforward. I felt supported, even when I asked for a few late-stage changes. I'm very pleased with how this book turned out and grateful to Kelsay Books for publishing *Each Bearing Out.*

You have a full-length poetry collection forthcoming this spring. Can you tell me more about The Way Land Breaks?

Each Bearing Out is a collection of my early mothering poems. In *The Way Land Breaks,* I use time—human and geological—as both anchor and engine. These poems have a wider scope: the Idaho

foothills of my childhood, my experience as a flight attendant, my relationship with my mother and sons, and the distances between.

"Raising Glaciers" and "Fine Lines" are included in *The Way Land Breaks.* "Good Housekeeping" has a similar theme—what it is to be living through, and raising children in, a time of such upheaval and loss, to know that life as it is now, for most of us, will not hold. There has been such a constant tumult these last several years—political, social, environmental. The question, for me, is still a constant: How do we mother these children toward a future we can't even begin to fathom? How do we, ourselves, live?

Can you tell me more about motherhood as a theme in your work?

Motherhood is both why I stopped writing, and why I started again. When my oldest was a baby, I was still writing fiction. But the multidimensional pulls of mothering, working, writing—I couldn't get them all to work for me. I admire the people who can keep going. But I had to set writing down for a long time. I wish I'd given myself more grace; I think I would have returned to writing a lot sooner.

That said, when I did return to writing, I found the intensity of poetry matched my experience of the intensity of motherhood. I can step into a poem for an hour, or less, and rearrange the world of it. My life so often feels like a blur, as if I'm standing knee deep in a swift moving stream of their growing up. My poems become rocks I can grab hold of from the streambed.

What would you tell mothers who want to find more time for writing?

Give yourself grace. More time comes, sometimes in seasons. My only trick is a terribly boring one: I get up really early. I try to free write a few pages every day, much like Julia Cameron suggests in *The Artist's Way.* That time and those pages add up. But I'm in a season now when my kids need a lot from me. The urgency is there, but I've got more grace for myself now. Or I try to have more.

Recently, I spoke with a writer several years ahead of me in life, her son married and grown. She told me women can actually have everything, just not at the same time. It was what I needed to hear.

In 2004, you earned an MFA from Bennington College. What is the most important thing you've learned in your writing practice that you did not *learn from your MFA?*

Perseverance. How to take the smallest of steps, and then the next slight shuffle forward, even with no one watching. Or maybe it's acceptance, of work not being perfect but maybe ready anyway, of a poem or story or process that takes the time it takes.

Would you explain why you were drawn to witness literature?

It has urgency. That idea that I cannot *not* write this, or tell this, that *listen to me!* Witness literature offers the intensity of the gaze, that burning. But also, as often, the need to come at something sideways, that simmer just beneath a narrative, whether it's hurt or power or injustice or an experience so beyond you. The way Lot's wife looked back. That innate human need to connect, to bear witness.

For me, Coleridge's *Rime of the Ancient Mariner* was my first and perfect example of witness literature. But witness literature also makes up so much of the poetry I love. Think Audre Lord, Adrienne Rich—Anna Akhmatova: "I stand as witness to the common lot,/survivor of that time, that place." I now see witness literature less as a niche and more the work we are all doing, or trying, to do.

Your 2005 award-winning essay "You Can't Even Remember What I'm Trying to Forget" describes your experience of being in the air as a flight attendant during 9/11. How did witness literature help you understand and create meaning from this experience?

I struggled to process my experience, struggled to find my way in. *Safekeeping* by Abigail Thomas was a map for me, and *The Boys of*

Summer 2023

My Youth by Jo Ann Beard. I gave my essay as a speech to my Bennington classmates, and, in many ways, that felt more like the catharsis than the writing of it did. That connection. That moment of being heard. After and since the essay was published, the response of my coworkers to my words feels binding—and full of meaning—as if I've been able to speak, a little, for and to their own experiences.

In your essay, you pose the questions: "How much of our return {from trauma} depends on the availability of our own voice? The ability to make both the memory and the human endure in the 'normal life' of return?" Do you think that, when an author is writing about something that has significant emotional relevance for them, there is a tension between their desire for catharsis and their ability to make good art? Or do the two go hand in hand?

For me, the two do go hand in hand. Of course, there is always tension. Too much feeling (or too much distance) can blur and blind us from seeing what is sentimentality vs. what is sentiment. Maybe trauma or significant emotional relevance offers the resonance needed to take our individual experience and expand it to the universal, or, a story that *must be* told.

What would you tell people who want to write about very emotional experiences they've had but hold back from fear that their work will come across as melodramatic, selfish, or simply too vulnerable?

I don't think we can know how our work will come across—that part is out of our hands once we let a poem, or story, or essay go into the world. So, I would say embrace it: be selfish, melodramatic and, especially, vulnerable. Write it. If writing the whole is too much, start with details, the smallest possible detail: a button, a bird wing, a dog's tail. Natalie Goldberg's books are fabulous at encouraging this. Same with Anne Lamott's *Bird by Bird.* One of my teachers, Amy Hempel, once said, and I'm paraphrasing: "There are no new things, just new ways into the old things." For me, with my 9/11 essay in particular, I leaned hard on using tangibles, particulars—about that day, my job, small moments—and that somehow anchored me enough to reach toward the bigger things, the universals beyond me and my own experience.

Your essay also speaks about the desire to "move on" from national traumas. As the title suggests, this often involves forgetting, whether this is intentional or unintentional. Do you see America's response to the Covid-19 pandemic as similar to the response to 9/11?

I think we are all exhausted. Forgetting or moving on from things is an understandable survival tactic. We are all out of bandwidth. One thing I haven't seen written about was the relief so many mothers felt in the initial phase of lockdown because it lifted the fear/stress so many of us carry constantly about school shootings. A lot of people ignored or forgot that our "normal" wasn't really working all that well either.

There was, and still is, a lot of "remembering" 9/11. America's response to Covid is dissimilar in that so many of us moved, or were led, so swiftly toward denial. Some of that happened with 9/11 but not to the scale or fallout that's happened with Covid. For a time, 9/11 brought so many of us together. Covid kept us apart.

My family and I have autoimmune issues that complicated our vulnerability. One of my best friends was a home health nurse working long days in a yellow rainsuit and duct tape because she didn't have PPE equipment. The calls to get back to normal came so swiftly and so vehemently, we missed another chance to reckon with ourselves as citizens—the way we do things, the way we care for ourselves, others and, especially, the most vulnerable among us. The experience of this disease was so wide and so varied—I'm not sure most of us want to process, or remember. Or maybe we just don't know how yet. Maybe someone writing right now will find a way to show us the way through.

Rebecca Brock
Raising Glaciers

If you look you can trace
the path of us. Measure snow pack
with your eyes: before and before and now
streams weep down mountain waterfalls,
the face of stone scarred and pocked
and jagged—no change goes smoothly.
I have been trying to show my sons
how to name—loss—and is it betrayal
to give them such language
in a world shifting
toward flashpoint
and heat?
What else is it to be human—
I run out of words to answer
their gaze, drive them to mountains,
give them landscape, offer
this disappearing world
as if it is one long gasp
of oh and awe, and see—do you see?
I am raising glaciers—lost causes, boys
with too soft hearts who know not to take
stones or approach wildlife, who know
how to name what is here, what is lost
if we can't name it.
Maybe the earth knows
the sun is too much—
and, anyway, catches
all the light it can.

First place in the 2022 Women's Poetry Contest

Rebecca Brock

A Rock Is a Rock Is a Rock

You got your feelings hurt at school, again,
you tell me seriously
that you feel a heartbeat
thump thump thunking
in your pet rock, you swear you can.
I say it's your own heartbeat,
in your palm, hammering.
I am straddling dinner
and your brother's baseball game—
and you try to explain
how your best friend tried to make you
throw the stupid thing away.
I say I told you not to take it to school,
I told you, over and over,
a rock is a rock is a rock.
I almost say, out loud, *baby*
sometimes you're just too much
but your breaths are coming hard,
your small chest heaves—love,
there is nothing weak about you.
I turn the stove off.
You let me hug you,
the pulse of you
barely surface deep.
When you let me hold him,
Rocky is still warm.
You believe in so many things,
even me.

Previously published in Whale Road Review *and* Each Bearing Out *(Kelsay Books, 2022)*

Rebecca Brock
Good Housekeeping

She keeps trying to get her house in order
pretending with the rest of them
that the sun won't melt the earth,
that the seas won't burn, that the land
won't disappear under water or ice
or our own triggered destruction.
She keeps going back to the dishes,
to the meals, to washing the clothes,
to worrying over the state of the carpet
which is funny in a sad way
if you knew the state of her house—
the way the windows leak, the way the doors
have to be snugged closed, the way
they blow open anyway, with the slightest wind,
the cracks in the ceiling from settling or moisture
or just poor craftsmanship. She still decorates
for holidays, she still worries
over the tidiness of things, the nutrition of meals,
the state of the bathroom—of the toilet—
under assault by the misdirection
and lack of attention
of three males in one small house.
She is like some mad woman
straightening a frame during an earthquake,
righting a vase after a hurricane took off the roof.
She sees it is the season to behave so,
to live beside, within madness—
to mother through it.

Summer 2023

It is despair pushed off
to vacuum anyway, to make a decent meal,
to require everyone to sit. She is hoping
the children won't notice or remember the windows,
the carpets—the way the door won't shut.
She is desperate for their happiness
for their solidity, for them to make it
to some new place
she never will.

Previously published in Mom Egg Review *and* Each Bearing Out *(Kelsay Books, 2022)*

Rebecca Brock
Fine Lines

after Brené Brown

She reads that midlife is when the universe
puts its hands on you, draws you close
and says: *listen, I'm not fucking around.*
So she resets her shoulders,
squares them down her back,
and reminds herself without saying
to stand up straight.
Days feel tumultuous
and full of moment, that awareness of brevity
makes her begin to watch the sky—
to look up more, to see the path itself,
even the way it turns.
Walking the dog becomes an excuse
for walking the self.
Something always hurts,
sometimes a shoulder, sometimes a back, or a hip—
sometimes the brain as though weighted
as though shaded with loss and bewilderment
and sometimes the heart—
beats get noticed, the breaths
prodded by the mind
as deep ins and outs.
She's learned it's normal to feel despair
at this or any age. Also rage.
After all she is doing the impossible.
Anybody that's paying attention knows
about upkeep and loss, the constant roil
and change of the body, the heart.

Forthcoming in The Way Land Breaks *Sheila-Na-Gig Editions (2023)*

Rebecca Brock

A Friend Texted to Interrupt This Poem

for Sarah

She asked if I was seeing the sunrise
and so I stopped writing, left my desk
and wandered into the backyard
to see the sky lit through
with clouds so pink
even the grey blue half of the sky
was tinged like a reflection.
There are no words here
just a gathering. A hold.
There is nothing to do
but breathe, maybe gratitude
maybe prayer, maybe just
that breath—from my tender
body, outside my fragile
house—the birds singing
from their fragile bodies,
the sky filling up and filling up
with color like a child
in love with pink colors the whole
of her picture—the grass, the dog,
the trees, even the sky:
pink and pink and pink.
A ridiculous color.
And yet I stand here
knowing friendship
holds me as much as any house might,

Summer 2023

as much as any skin or poem
or wandering. My feet bare
on stone, the dog in the doorway
head cocked—the rows and rows
of houses still asleep
and that sky—
in spite of all
I was trying to write
about being temporary,
about the ruins of us—
that sky.

Nikki Ummel
Walking My Niece Home

We veer off the path,
        head for the trees,
    knee-deep in pine straw.

My niece launches herself
           from the Radio Flyer,
her feet crunching pine-needles.

She sinks her hands into sharp pinecones.
    They become missiles,
        bomb the thick straw for enemy ships.

Look! I cry,
    pointing to the looming trees: *the pine cones*
                             have come so far.

She jumps, flaps her hands open and closed.
We have to put them back,
        she says. *Their mommy will miss them.*

Clutching pinecones in her too-small palms,
    she hugs them to her body:
        A child, far from home. Mother,
    unreachable.

Summer 2023

Sharp   distance.   My sister,
sheathed in stiff sheets & soft lights,
pink nails painted by hospice nurses.
She is two.   The world is still kind.

I tell her,   *some things can't*

come home.

She takes a pinecone, shoves it
in my pocket, deep.

She says,
We will make a home for them.

Second place in the 2022 Women's Poetry Contest

Kristen Holt-Browning
Window Seat

It's raining again and I am furious for snow, staring out windows, longing to witness poor animals in the woods beyond the yard, and imagine myself paw-cold and snout-lost. The fact is it troubles me, although I joke about it, how quickly I would end out there: a starving, unwashed day or two, and I'd already be too tired to shelter myself, never mind dig a proper hole to lie in. In here, where windows lock firmly, the risk is that weather becomes an aesthetic accessory, a charming backdrop to a cup of tea. But there's the half-eaten mole the cat brought home. He has a relationship to place that makes my guts lurch when he slinks toward the forest in his lion bones. Also, the shaggy deer—I know I make them nauseous, the human smell of me repulsive in their noses. I may be silk-robed at the window, lavendered and saged, but I don't forget the scars I wear, the borders where I tore to blood, exposing bone and babies. Not to imply that I'm wounded. I live in a fresh house unburdened by history. I have enough meat to survive. No blood. Only candlelight, which does a poor job of illuminating the forest, the hungry animals in the dark.

Honorable mention in the 2022 Women's Poetry Contest

Lori Howe

A New Law of Liquids in Flight

for Patrick

At the deep kitchen sink, I blow a handful of iridescent foam
across morning's uncharted kitchen to watch it sail
like a lit cloud through sunlight, to see it pillow
golden as raclette dripping garlicky and fine from seeded rye
toasted caramel over open flame, to watch it wisp linen-white
and clean as an egret through cool air at sunrise,
to willow gently as a dancer's tulle in the first lemony quiet of day.
Oh, we have missed this, I think—missed knowing
that liquids can be anything, anything, while in flight;
missed knowing that desire is solid, liquid, and gas
all at once, shifting from amber to nectarine and back to oxygen.
Oh, my love, the heart is not a scientist, but a container
meant to leak a little, a jar of honey on its side, a slow streaming
    out;
once freed from the glass ribs of logic, its contrails spooning us
    this
fleeting, sticky mouthful of sweetness where we lie together
in the fragrant shade of wild pinyons and clementines.

Honorable mention in the 2022 Women's Poetry Contest

Summer 2023

Jacqueline Coleman-Fried
Snowdrops This Year

I know I startled you
at the end of January, usually a time of ice
and misery in this part of the country.
But the soil was soft after a few
rain-soaked weeks. So I uncurled, picked
the garden that faces south all day,
and popped up. My plump buds, like drops
of milk on green stems, slender as grass,
thrilled you—is winter really over?
I surprised you again after two arctic days,
when my head bowed like I was dying—
in the next chiffon breeze, I straightened
as if I hardly noticed. I risked my life to pierce
your darkness. Legend says an angel
consoled Eve with the gift of me.

Mitzi Dorton

When Robins Lift the Veil

When robins lift the veil
From winter's field of froth
To birth blue eggs and banner grounds
And signs of winter, scoff

With wonderment I shed my wraps
Under popcorn-blossom trees
The sun sprays down on clothesline sheets
Ghosts wrestling in the breeze

Little bells on hyacinths
Ring sounds for fairies' ears
The pansies twirl in cartwheels
The tulips toast us, "Cheers!"

My imagination from my youth
Takes over as I please
Daffodils are telephones
For butterflies and bees

I'm pleased the winter sidewalks
That screak beneath the fluff
No longer need a shovel's blade
And smell of rain and earth

Summer 2023

I happily peek in fairy doors
Twisted trunks of woodland crews
And pretend that they are storied rooms
As cardinals dart in twos

They say it's luck to see them
Like a visit from the dead
A new life start announcement:
No winter threats to dread!

Hilary Biehl
Nestlings

Imagine being born up high, aware
first of a blur
of blossoms. Your whole nursery
is wallpapered with sky.

The winds are cold,
unsettling, but petaled
spaciousness is all you know.
The bough

tends constantly to bend
and sway. The ground
is theoretical, an unreal rumor of solidity;
that heady

drop is just one distance among
distances. Your mother's song
stops when you ask her what "down" means.
She flies away. Then come the rains,

blown at sharp angles to your nest.
Each gust
feels like a loss—you learn
to worry that she won't return.

But just as suddenly, it stops. The sun
appears again:
pale, powerless, but lovely. And she's back,
a white worm in her beak.

Summer 2023

Juan Pablo Mobili
The Doe Led Her Fawn Under the Bush

The doe led her fawn under the brush
the moment she sensed my presence.
Her eyes stared at me softly but
her shoulders seemed to rally for reinforcements,

and I felt misunderstood
picked on for no good reason,
profiled,
sadness that leaves no fingerprints.

How could I explain that to the doe?
How could I convince a mother
she did not have to worry about her child?

After all, I could not recall a single time
that pleading to my mother to "be happy"
did not turn into a failure we hid under the brush.

I could tell from the stillness in her eyes
that to her I was the enemy,
and given the tragic history of deer
I had no chance.

Daniel Lusk

A Map of the World

This infant footprint in the files
might show the road laid out for her.
Or chart her river and its influences.

The work of a child is to tend the wild grasses.
To learn the sunburnt smell of dragonflies.
To love deep spaces in the fern beds.
To separate petals of iris and rose.

Remember the wise one
was not just any mackerel peddler.
How might a woman balance
the light outside and the light within?

In a choir of a thousand voices, be silent.
In a crowd of shining faces, be a shadow.
On fasting day, turn from your mother's kiss.

Think how a long line of people and horses
wound across this land, past the edge of the trees,
past the line of mountains
toward the place they last saw buffalo.

Some days the soul flies out and the body with it,
trailing after,
the way a flamingo carries its feet in flight.

Summer 2023

Work to know equally sun and shadow
and there will be plenty.
Pay attention where you go
and where you lie down.

It is said that madness is a foreign country
where one might gain favor as Aaron did
if one's walking stick bursts into flower.

Previously published in The Shower Scene from Hamlet *(Maple Tree Editions, 2017)*

Daniel Lusk
Air in the Lost Decade

Now here is something I had thought
never to see again—eyes of a sleepwalker
clouded with dream.

Fog billows up
from the ash grove, obscuring
all but the naked feet
of girls playing croquet on the lawn.

A boy leaps shouting from a cliff
above the silt-slow river,
alive every second he is falling.

Awash in mist,
the eye of the setting sun glimmers
like the salmon's back in its violent surging,

or the hem of the somnambulist's gown
where it brushed the wet grass.

Previously published in Kissing the Ground *(Maple Tree Editions, 1999)*

Ray Malone
Sonnet 141

Hum a little. Home's not far.
Stars or no stars. The dark is the dark.
The hedges hold no echoes. None but yours.
Every edge to be trod your edge. *Say it.*

For every sound a source. Somewhere.
Hold on to the least of things. A light.
A litter of things a shade each. A shift.
Issuing into your eye. Your appetite.

There's measure in the merest of. Meanest of.
A music of grit against grit. The sand.
Memories of. The stir of particles.
A poem wearing itself away. In time.

Something might be made of it. A hum.
Who's to know how far from home it is.

Peycho Kanev
Quietly

I pass through the street,
I pass through the park,
I pass through the city to the last lamp,
the last light in the darkness,
only the moon embraces me,
she puts her white hands over my mouth
and tells me to keep quiet and watch.
And I hear the rotten murmur of the ages,
and the false promises of the sea
for serenity and infinity;
the dark is everywhere and it is absurd,
just because it exists, like you and me,
like all living things in the night;
and Baudelaire is still dead,
and the beer is already stale,
and the icons in the church sleep,
suppressed by their holiness,
let them be cursed,
just like this dark night is,
which no candle can penetrate,
but I still managed to get to all this,
to the end of the light, to the visible beginning
of mortality,
and I know that on a night like that
I will go as I came,
quietly.

Michele Rappoport
Don't Talk to Me

I wake up thirsty then remember I no longer have a mouth. I think of all the other mouths still loose in the world and bar the door. Mouths running sleek as ferrets with bodies like tails themselves, no one knows where they begin or end. The mouth that carries a pen but never writes. The mouth that takes a slap for a kiss. The treacherous mouth, darkest factory, teeth black as smokestacks. The mouth I found in the park, the one that followed me home, asked to be petted, took a knife to my pillows. The one that lured me like candy but tasted like gunpowder. Your mouth, your words, all relative, like a weed. The times I pulled at it so my garden would be perfect.

Summer 2023

Al Ortolani
Shooting at Rabbits

Early dawn, the cockcrow is light
through flint glass, a mercury-silvered
mirror. All that is illuminated tilts
to the left of sun, behind rooftops,
behind the curve of the horizon.
The smallest birds are flickers
in the highest branches, maples
and oaks, a poplar. The fence
between our yards, weather-worn,
lists with repair. I am the only
one up so early, not a light
in a window, the pastel paste
of suburbia deepening with the
approach of rain. We are practiced
at sheltering in place, ankle deep
in the retreat from traffic,
from shopping carts, from the
hand sanitizer displays, already
picked to bone, already gone
the way of an uncle, like my mother's
Uncle Bill, the one with the pencil thin
mustache, who once on a country road,
pulled a .22 single from the floorboards,
swung it up in front of my face, and fired
down the crossroad, dust skipping
where he aimed, a rabbit
darting into a stand of tall grass
without a scratch, none
the worse, none the better.

Summer 2023

Today, I wait for time to pass.
Morning, rabbit-eared, hesitates
to meet the day, a train in the distance,
and the neighbor, if watching,
parts the curtain
with the barrel of her nose.

Andrew Mauzey
Detour

When you wake early,
start your day with a detour.
Follow the greenbelt
to the park. Hear rakes scrape

sand. See dogs dip and dive
for tennis balls. Hear an old man
sing "Kilgary Mountain," notes
grinding through his throat

like seedlings
pushing through cracks
of concrete, their yellow buds
stretching good morning yawns.

Walk beside a row of forsythia
bushes. Listen to the swish
and splash of soles and heels
dropping in and out of puddles

made by sprinklers. See squirrels
climb bark and hear bicycles
zip like whispers telling secrets
to the road. See the shapes

of clouds—chopsticks
lifting hair into a pulled-back bun
and the soft, billowy texture
of sheep grazing the sky.

When night falls, walk.
Stop beneath the dull light
of the Laundromat.
Watch the lamplight paint

the blinds, and see your breath
gather like clouds. Notice
shadows braid the street
black and gray, the checkered

strips gleaming like bone.
Feel the cold air sharpen
your senses in night's dull
valley. Hear birds sing

with open beaks toward
lingering lamps. See them
spin air straight legged
and free. Notice how

they rest beside the corner
of a locked newsstand,
twitching their heads
until they fly again. Air

ripping past wings, their songs
like long silver ribbons
strangling the dark, a kind
of touch to shock on contact.

Maximilian Speicher
The Mirrored Sky

Beyond the mountains, in the valley, far
from any major town, to both sides of
the little river spanned by bridges here
and there, surrounded once by pristine forest
now dying due to climate change (a fact
so grave how could one dare express it through
a metaphor?)—there lies, so very lonely,
a village, barely thousand souls in size.
A century ago (three hundred years
in village-time), a ribbon made from steam
was dragged along the valley. Take a stroll
on it, through catacombs and vaults, in green
and brownish colors, borne by ancient granite.
The kind of place where, off the beaten path,
you'd find an empty bottle from an old,
incorporated brewery, the beer
of which has long been drunk, entirely.
Inhale the dense blue air, then take a right.
Behind a meadow lies, asleep and out
of sight, a secret riverbend, reserved
for those you deem the most important in
your life. The water: crystal-clear and cold.
A book by Stephen Hawking lies atop
a table in the meadow. Someone must
have left it there—for you?
                              The Universe in
a Nutshell

Summer 2023

Dusk arrives, and as the sun
begins to set, between the leaves of grass
appears a light, and then another one,
and then another one, until they form
a Milky Way, as if the sky were mirrored.

Adina Polatsek
Houston

There are bats here, when the sun
goes down, and cactus plants
with big leaves, and ant-mounds
in the grass. The summer grows
sunflowers and blackberries. I still
don't love the cement-flat streets
and the bright lights against the sky,
but I walk it easily. My bed
is soft, and there is coffee
in the kitchen. I wonder why
I say no to everything I want.

Glenn Irvin
Night Wind

The night wind wails across an anxious sky
and leaves the distant stars in disarray.
It whips the surface of the pond awry
and taunts the creeping edge of coming day.

It sits astride a naked limb and stirs
with savage laugh. It whispers deep desires
and raises feelings long left undisturbed
that fan the embers of implacable fires.

Its fingers pluck the notes of fervid fancies
and stroke with subtle touch the strings of meaning.
It strums the chords of forgotten fantasies
that sound the blue nocturne of my being.

The night wind's song infects my naked soul—
my spirit aches to feel its burning rhythm.
Its voice enraptures with a wanton call,
and I must travel with him.

Summer 2023

Jeannie E. Roberts

A Sestina for the Dog-Day Cicada

N. canicularis

As nymphs rise from the blue-black depths of Earth,
light reveals the abstract radiance of life.
Aboveground, they ascend trees, shed their shells.
Here, wings plump for the upcoming courtship,
bodies change, mature into refined being.
The males' drum-like plates vibrate for a mate.

Does the buzz quality matter in a mate?
Should it yearn with a burn the hot days on Earth?
Do females fancy the exact being?
Or is it the right hum that begets life?
Is there a feeling of pleasure in courtship?
Are there shudders and shakes, quakes to the shell?

Eggs laid in branches don shiny, white shells.
Larvae hatch, evolve, years later they mate.
Tree sap's their steadfast fare, a food court(ship).
Youth feed, fatten, then fall to meet the earth.
Young nymphs develop an underground life,
where they dig tunnels, eat into being.

Does the beginning begin with the being?
Or does the beginning begin shell to shell?
Can living midst the depths be a good life?
Is there teenage angst? Do they scan for a mate?
When nymphs emerge, is there a party on Earth?
O praised be the dog-day parties of courtship!

Summer 2023

Summer love woos with the sounds of courtship.
The buzzing months pitch loudness of being.
"Power saws" sing from the treetops of Earth.
As adults display their brown and green shells,
dawn to dusk drones in the limbs for a mate.
Like tinnitus, their ringing calls to life.

Is it worth the wait to create new life?
Downunder, are nymphs pondering courtship?
If so, could they be visualizing a mate?
Do nymphs find vitality in being?
Or, at times, do they feel like an empty shell?
Do they see purpose in each phase on Earth?

The air of courtship blesses the bounty of Earth.
As life unfolds in the blue-black depths of a shell,
the thrums for a mate brighten the cycle of being.

Robert Knox
Wild Rice

Take me to the place where the wild rice grows,
to the Indian rice and the muddy toes,
the fatty seed that the wild fowl knows,
take me where the wild rice grows.

Take me to the place where the shadows fall,
to the August mists and willows tall,
the slow fish nibble on toes so small,
take me where the shadows fall.

Take me to the place where the lovers meet,
to the silent dawns and the rain-washed feet,
to the mingled dreams of a lost retreat,
take me where the lovers meet.

Anna Evas

Flora's Psalm 1:3

The magnolia's white doves
lift ecstatic eyes, atomize

the summer air with
lemon-honeysuckle breath,

each wing a votary
waxed as a yellow moon

circling a turret
with many windows

torchlike in the fall,
fruit on the sills.

Anna Evas

Narcissus and Echo in the Afterlife

The pool by the sycamores tightened
like skin around a wound.

He kissed the disturbance,
though his likeness was nowhere

in it. Still,
the water tasted warm,

even medicinal,
when a half-familiar voice

lifted his head.
Robed in saffron mist,

singing her own name, Echo
had decamped from the caves.

The nymph's emergence
a trail through the trees,

he left his mirror,
the clearing just ahead.

Alexander Etheridge
Promise

The last time I saw you
we walked down the road a little
and you had a scent of
fresh oranges and
something finer
I can't describe here

You put white elder flowers
in your red hair
as you let me into your
kinder world
with a pure note
never heard before

I think of how your hand
brushed against mine
By your gaze I was
cleansed
in the eyes of Heaven
I want to give you a pure word

never spoken before
because everything I have seems
like a peasant's gift
I'll never be enough
but when we walk together I'm
more than I ever was

Jeffrey Thompson
Tracks

1.
Alphabets fluttered
between the cottonwoods.
Punctuation marks
wriggled in muddy pools.
The history lessons
of the exposed clay buttes,
the encyclopedia of sky!

2.
And here we are, you and I,
leaving smudges on the mirror,
thumbprints on darkened screens.

3.
Roll down the window, please.
Let's listen again to the bison
as they tear off mouthfuls of grass,
chewing with infinite slowness along the roadside
like creatures at home.

Summer 2023

Bailey Parker
Villanelle no. 2

Oh, don't make me make it plain
Sanctuary lies between the lines
Speak my language, sing my name

Your voice falls like a gentle rain
On the tin roof of my near rhymes
Oh, don't make me make it plain

In your eyes, I find a poet's pain;
To live and die a thousand times
Speak my language, sing my name

Look at my hands, at their ink stains
Every word I write builds you a shrine
Oh, don't make me make it plain

Crack my skull, comb my brain
Break my ribs, betray God's designs
Speak my language, sing my name

Instead, I watch you drift out of frame,
Out of reach, like all that's divine
Oh, don't make me make it plain
Speak my language, sing my name

Elizabeth Galewski
Sublimations

You are a splinter.
I can't let you stay.
But digging you out
would be even more painful.
I wrap myself around your sharp points.
Now I know why oysters form pearls.

     * * *

I cut the splinter out
by writing it down:

> After five weeks of silence,
> as I walked around the pool,
> you—bent nearly double, leaning against and
> partially hidden by a lifeguard chair—
> called my name.
>
> You said you lost my number,
> called yourself an idiot, and
> ran your hands through your hair.
> You put my number in your phone
> and texted me
> while I stood beside you.

If you read this poem,
please see here raised
a monument.
Now I'll never forget.

Laura Vitcova

Felled

My arms once covered in needles
like a porcupine, now boughs

sweeping the dirt beneath your feet.
I pine for you, I am willing

to be eaten by mold, I am letting
worms bring water to lobes

breathing crimson rivers,
no longer exhaling sulfur.

I am as indifferent to termites
as I am to woodpeckers,

but to you, dear, there is no cap.
I have surrendered all thresholds.

My roots no longer hold onto dry soil,
gale and gravity have instructed

me to fall now and I am
kissing the earth over and over again.

Amy DeBellis

Vesuvius Pulse

I think that if I kissed you, it would taste
like rust or moss. Something that forms
when no one is looking.

You teach me how to load a gun,
how to hunt duck and rabbits and quaking deer,
but I long for something larger, I dream
of bears
      boars
            bison:

bodies colossal
pierced and falling to earth.

In the evening the fields turn leaden
gray like my parents. My father dying
sunk full of morphine.

No deer here, only a neighbor's cat
slinking through wheat thinking herself
unseen. I watch us watching her, everything
the color of ghosts.
Everything with a heart fair game.

Soon the woods will turn murky and raucous with dark.
You smile, a trap twisting shut.

Summer 2023

Daniel Brennan
A Ghazal Betrays Me

I'm watching you watching him. This watchtower night,
    it whistles back,
bad luck. All this to say: we both find ourselves defined
    by our hunger.

Years ago, watching in the dark, I said I loved you. Not
    with words, but how
can that matter now? Can I not speak solely through my
    echoing hungers,

the impossible friction of want on my tongue? Watch
    this poem, it's an anagram for
see me. See our lips seconds and still decades away
    from collision, twisting in hunger.

Watch me, see me sinking into a bed, into daylight, into
    your arms. Sinking
under the weight of knowing you all these years and
    carrying hunger

like a second skin. At these parties of friends of friends
    of friends, we move against
the current. Against the night. I move because if I don't,
    my hunger

will bury me alive. Yes, I'm watching you watching him.
    I'm watching all the ways
you can love a man in the dark. Yes, watch me. See me.
    This sinking. This hunger.

Megan Wildhood

Evaporation

Sun burns like a neighbor's judgment
even in its soft peek down,
giving away its diamonds to the sea.
Sea doesn't know that this is for free,

so, in return, it parses and parts with pieces
of itself small enough to scale
the wavy cords of light, hoping
to make it all the way back to the sun.

Now each—the many beaded bodies of water
and the bright twines linking
and lifting them—know what it is
to come completely apart in union.

Chris Dahl

Aubade: The Mock-Orange

A ghost lover lingers in the comforter's
hollow, even as I hear him rattling
through the house, his chains domestic.
Though he doesn't follow a gloomy path,
and I will find him if I rouse,

I lie in languor, savoring
the morning's veer
toward the physical: foliage rushed
through spring to fill the window
with crosshatched weirs of branch
that trap the flow of green

and hold it in suspense while flowers
foam: an immense, burgeoning wave readied
to cascade and bury May. The very moment
thrums on the cusp
between anticipation and the played-out

blossoms spent. Let sweetly
scented bowers of mock-orange cry
Love, return, because the present,
that quiescent, dandling sea, is rented
from time, and already
the white crests churn.

Don Niederfrank
Valentine Villanelle

Other things may well be true,
But this truth has come to me:
I get to be with you.

There were days that I now rue,
When I failed us miserably.
Other things that have been true.

Out from them a new "we" grew,
And daily we renew that "we."
I get to be with you.

We waltz, limp, and soft shoe,
And you get to be with me.
Another thing that is quite true.

Uncounted years now feel few.
Thus these days I clearly see:
I get to be with you.

So until the end's in view,
Whatever comes, we'll be.
And whatever else proves true,
I got to be with you.

Phil Huffy

Don't Look Back

Walk with me in our sublime direction
into the heartline where the future lies,
without the need for pause or introspection,
a journey without question or reprise.

Do not look too deep; you won't see clearly
the pathways that my footsteps may have tread,
for all I care to offer you, sincerely,
are features of a life now being led.

All those slings and arrows misdirected,
and any traumas that I may have known,
are simply pale penumbras now collected
and secrets best considered as my own.

Ginger Dehlinger
Soupe d'Amour

A savory potage
of languid days
and gluttonous nights
scooped from la cuvette
or sipped from a stiletto.

No mushrooms or legumes
in this steamy broth,
a moveable feast
seasoned with bones, blood
and skin of many colors.

La bonne soupe—
a buttery lusciousness
supped and slurped
till we lick the spoon,
crying for more.

Erica M. Breen

Sugarhouse Alchemy

Fragrance waltzes out to meet us
from between the heavy doors.
Through pillows of steam,
fire flashes, hinges moan, bubbles murmur and rise;
we breathe the blood of trees.

Flames turn the syrup thick and amber,
we stir and skim and stoke and sample,
as if we could taste the trees' vast wisdom in the sap
and know the future.

Year after year, we gather sap, feed the fire,
tend the boil. Years upon years of this same work,
piled up like the sugarwood in the shed,
poured like sap into the pans,
our detritus boiled away.

Year after year, the sweet essence thickens
what we have chosen—

a taste of God lingers,
shimmers golden across
our tongues and seasons.

Kelley White

Dog Days

Today my heart sits heavy as unrisen bread, as stones
And I turn to you in anger though the anger is my own
And our home sits dark though birdsong waits just past the
    cabin door—
why don't I sing why don't you ask kind questions anymore?

Summer 2023

Samuel Samba
Hardened in no small way

I preserve the stonefruit to harden myself,
& they in turn preserve my delicate life: squeezable blessing of
mouthwatery vitamin—chowed in raw silence.

I study their shelf life & it walks me through patience,
from ripening into a terrible sweetness.

while talking to a therapist, I mouth my secrets
& they peel open without my consent.

he hands me a handkerchief, plead that I weep halfway
to make room for a client. after which, he splits my palm apart—
translating my grief in sugary accent.

I raise my tongue & it becomes a burden.
language, silvering in the corner of my lung as one hundred
    hatching pain.

in my youth, traders question me about my origin
& I point the space in between ripening and rot,
question me about death, & I fold as though the word
blades through air—to harvest me.

the makeshift kiosk where I own my smaller needs, brimming with
    juiciness.

Summer 2023

a catechist once lured my pagan self into visiting the chapel.
in lieu of firstfruit, he palms me a kaki
& I misjudge his caregiving for innocence.
even the best of us interprets kindness the wrong way.
once, my lover gifted me a Sharon fruit.
I grew wild with thirst. ignored its naked sting, ravaging my
    tongue.
the peel of it—red with intention.
& with my lips ajar, I down the forest of grape.

the next week voices me into a nearby store in search of more,
& I found the long row of edible yellow, beckoning at me from a
    butcher's slab.

the grocer lets out a grin, peel out his palm—kneading a stonefruit.
I weigh my worth by each strike, & conclude: life deals us a
    deathblow.

here, am I. offshoot of grace, hardened in no small way.

Angela Hoffman

Look Through the Storms for the Flowers

after William Stafford, "Ask Me"

Sometime when there is a snowfall in late April,
ask me how I forgive all over again.
Yesterday I cut asparagus just hours old
after waiting three long years for it to live up to its promises.
In the cracks of the cement, a pansy emerged, all tender,
and there was the lacy moss thriving on top of a stone.
The hyacinth and daffodils, with little reason to believe,
were brave enough, despite the cold reception.
Even the forsythia hung out its prayer flags.
The spoils of last season were composted in my garden,
turned over and over into wisdom, and the spinach
made it through the long winter.
The sun rose when the world was still dark,
dressed again in her pinks.
There are black mulberries stains on my soles,
but just like the chartreuse buds,
I'll muster enough hope to forgive you for everything.

Jean Janicke

Life Gives You Lemons

My grandmother believed
in healing powers of sun
and lemons. We squeezed slices
for invisible ink, added heat
to see the secret. We juiced
our hair, hoping for highlights
painted by Texas sun. My mother
poured lemon water remedies, baked
lemon birthdays from Betty Crocker
boxes, painted the front door lemon
yellow on a beige suburban street.
She and her sisters ate lemons whole,
growing thick dimpled skin
over sharp zest within.

Bill Howell
August Song

Low, Quebec

Finally the goldenrod;
this day already absorbing
its own afterglow.

Drowsy bees dangle, resemble
last chances, lost visions,
the latest unborn dreams.

Becoming the moment, the moment
becomes something else: suddenly
everything's going to seed.

Green sparks & bleeds
mottles of darkening shadow
across the lengthening shade.

So what do we keep
having & forgetting to learn
or somehow miss?

What about taking care. That caring.
That carefulness with our lives
inside our latest seasons.

Jeremy Gadd
The Fragile Flower

Freedom grows in several varieties,
often cross-fertilizes and self-sows,
and, when compared to subjugation grey,
its blooms are colorful and vibrant.

Freedom's seeds float everywhere
like weightless, white dandelion puffs—
as light as liberty on sunny day—
they often waft over totalitarian walls

and tend to germinate wherever
they fall, allowing dissent,
freedom of choice, always
encouraging an independent voice.

But freedom is a fragile flower
requiring constant attention,
nurturing and protection
from encroaching weeds like

menacing despots or approaching
oppression; for freedom often
vacillates before a storm and,
sometimes, wilts when too warm.

Despite this, freedom's fragrance is
extremely rare, valuable beyond
compare, worth every effort to cultivate
—the alternative is to live in thrall,

emasculated by mind control,
enslaving serf's shackles or
restraining chains and iron ball,
which, surely, are anathema to all?

Leslie Schultz
Consanguinity

There are hundreds of red flowers
in my garden: bee balm,
geraniums, red sunflowers,
gerbera daisies from Africa,
cultivars called Mercury Rising
and Chinese Red Dragon and
so many kinds of zinnias.

Hummingbirds soar to them,
thrumming with excitement, hope.

Today, I see a bee probing
the heart of an open helianthus,
its iridescent green head
framed by deep scarlet petals.
Little sweat bee, are not you
and I sisters? And all these
red faces our own giddy aunts?

Summer 2023

Leslie Hodge
Escape

Open the door to let the dog out,
a hummingbird flies in too fast to see,
then the tap-tap-tap-tap of a needle beak
on the inside of the window, the whir of wings.

I gasp, snap the dish towel and drop
a porcelain teacup—it shatters.

> *No hummingbird has made it inside before,*
> *although there have been a few other birds.*
> *And a lizard. Wasps and bees, naturally.*
> *Once a rattlesnake who sulked*
> *under the bookcase until animal control*
> *arrived with their loop on the long stick*
> *and a big burlap bag—bored and businesslike.*

Collapsed on the windowsill
palm-sized ruby-throated.
So still, I think he has died,
toothpick bones broken—
but no, he flurries and smashes
himself against the glass again.

Fast and frantic, I wrench open the window,
tear off the screen—and he escapes.

> *I know that longing,*
> *to be among the birds-of-paradise.*

Previously published in In Parenthesis

Douglas Cole
Sunday on a Whim

Squirrels are eating the insulation.
The back door is wide open—
but the black cloud has passed over.
Why so sullen, face on the wall?
You need a strategy to get from here
to the car. It's quiet now, but any moment
the bullets will be flying.

I slice a sliver of self and say,
you go live the mid-century modern
with pool and sound view
and more rooms than you'll ever need,
while I eat roots and walk under palms
head exploding like a dandelion seed.

Look it up, you'll find nothing
on the filmmaker, one movie out,
a solitary prayer that won't burn down,
but watery images drift into your dream
even when you're driving home
under an animated fishbone sky.

At least I call it home: beach shack lean-to,
all I need is a little fire, night music,
and the hieroglyphics of the waves—
sun door I slide through to bring you
these glimpses, these bits of other world
eyes like a gallery vision in a gum wall
you can put your concentration to and see.

79

Summer 2023

Sunset Cliffs to Golden Gardens—
ragged fractal edge, a thing you feel
and hear—no wonder this looks familiar:
shaggy trees, birds, hillside sloughing
water to the slough, deck top rolling
mist assuming another day,
parting like a game show curtain
revealing what we've won.

Summer 2023

Barbara Anna Gaiardoni
Untitled

long trip
down a lazy river
electric grasshoppers

Miguel Alfonso Ramos
coastwalk

muddy gray beach
    connects
to gray sea
    connects
to gray sky
      each merging into the other

the sun
a silver coin
burns faintly
behind the gauze of the sky
    a blind eye
    searching for rest

stranded rocks
above the tideline
reflect the wave's susurrus,
the gull's plaintive cries

herons
    geese
        terns
fill the landskymud
of the endless twilight

strong brown smiles
walk beside me
leading the way
into the heart of
this land

Summer 2023

Mary Beth Hines
Bloody Mary Morning

Measure, mix,
stir, sip,
and boom:

      we're twenty-six
      again!

Sliding glass
      doors open

to rumbling,
sultry air.

      The beach
           breeze kicks up.

I seize
his easy hand.

      We careen past
      the battened pool,
           shuttered sun
           umbrellas.

Catch storm
waves buffeting

      the arms-wide,
           palms-up shore.

Garret Keizer

Same-Old, Same-New

We think it is routine that makes us dull,
same-old-same-old that turns us old before
our time, whereas it is our bountiful
distractions that make the daily office bore

us till we're bores ourselves. The benefit
of conscious habit is to take us deep
where otherwise we'd go but wide. A nitwit
fancies finding buried treasure with a leap

from port to port and bed to bed, like a dog
in a parking lot piss-marking the tires.
He sniffs a bum and calls it dialogue,
calls pushing a button engineering the wires.

The constancy of the breakers rolling in to you
is what strews the low-tide sand with the new.

Jason L. Martin
Sunfish

as if hummingbirds fell into the lake,
grew gills, mutated fins from wings;
their songs splash in the murky waters
and their colors radiate through algae.
a rainbow, stretched across the sky,
broke into pieces and became sunfish.

I dip in my hand, schools of sunfish
race to hidden recesses inside the lake.
their wingéd counterparts span the sky,
the flocks swim in a wider sphere, wings
with more space to flutter, no nasty algae
lingering and stagnant in these bluer waters.

this morning, grandpa and I sit by the waters
and toss out baitless lines for the sunfish.
I help him skim away the film of algae
with a broom, uncovering the muddy lake.
I notice small brown feathers of bird wings
floating on the water's edge, as if the sky

kissed the lake last night, birds in the sky
passionately mating with fish in the waters.
grandpa says they once snipped pigeon wings
and used the feathers for pens. I lament sunfish
that hook their lips on grandpa's line, the lake
losing brilliant colors, replaced by more algae.

grandpa says when he was a boy he drank algae
soup for his fevers. I grin and stare into the sky,
as the sun lulls with the tiny currents on the lake.
the grand imaginations of a little boy: the water
and the sky like pieces of bread, birds and sunfish
like bits of rye, all the middle stuff with wings,

or legs in mine and grandpa's case. if birds without wings
have indeed mated with fish having no fins, the algae
would be like small green islands for the hybrid sunfish.
grandpa died today while he napped beside the water-sky:
I pulled his line to shore for him, and, as if these waters
felt the sky's adrenaline, I lifted a rainbow from the lake,

pieces of colored wings flapping up into the sky
told me that grandpa's waters, though harboring algae,
held a world full of sunfish in our own imaginary lake.

Diane Lee Moomey

Wearing Snakes

I let them wrap around my wrists, the sleek
green scales so like the bracelet, golden-linked,
that Mother wears to parties. So alike—
I close my eyes while wearing one and feel

the other. In summer's green beside the fence,
by long stems my father's mower doesn't
reach, I wait, place my wrist on mullein,
grasses, dock. They part. I intercept

and lift, feel it wrap. Snake will twine
around an arm, always: body taut
and steadying itself against a fall.
(Ruby tongue flicks in and out.) In my

own world I am, (ruby tongue tastes,)
the only little girl who wears snakes.

Erin Jamieson

Granny

I cracked open my bedroom window
July heat prickling my neck

My mother entered the room
and asked who I was talking to

Granny, I said, turning back
to my imaginary tea party

To this day I'm not sure
if it was all my imagination
or if, before I started questioning,
I knew how to listen

Tara Menon
Pact

The little red bird
high on the tree
voiced a shrill complaint,
then fluttered to a nearby tree,
dove down and disappeared.

Where did she go?
What was she going on about?

In the olden days, when people
were good, birds and folks
understood each other,
but now only ornithologists
know what the winged creatures mean,
and perhaps the wise corvids
guess what we say.

Imagine if I could have
conversed with that little red bird.
We could have exchanged complaints.
Made some kind of pact
with a red feather and strands of hair.
Every time we had a bad day,
one of us could have tweeted away.

Deborah J. Shore

At the Core

Magnets, gravity—within, without.
Our chests amass their density and flux,
a stiffening fire-melt, a shifting flood,
a moon that pulls blue billows black, profound.

The whole world pulses as both ear and mouth,
it greets our angsty chaos with a tug
whose giant heart's presumed dispassion lugs
a question mark. Are mundane chambers wound

with spirit, earth's red oxygen a mirror?
Do gold-veined rocks not map the crust-slip—grafts
now fused and filled with—substance of the Greater?

Our Center's a receiver, for all Nature
listens deeper, fluency inhered.
How swiftly stillness moves with silver sap.

Summer 2023

Susan Lendroth
Song of Wind, Song of Light

Wind chimes ring behind our house
in random harmony,
riffing with each hummingbird
and erratic bumblebee.
A glass dragon also sways there,
seeming mute while wind chimes sing,
but sunshine sparks cantos of light
from each iridescent wing.

Laurence de B. Anderson
A Fire in Eden

See, as here above, the
playing boughs, in wind,
the dancing unhampered,
burst of leaves couching summer's mass of flowers,
as we look up bedazzled, questioning everything,
with our strange eyes,
not belonging in this Eden.
Because we see this unrehearsed joy as
throngs of warriors, battle mimic, plot.
We humans.
But one day when the frost is on our lips
in the outermost unwarming,
we will remember
the opulent thrash of bloom, earth flaunting her silks,
and us, not belonging.

Summer 2023

Douglas MacDonald

Make Us Part of You

Beyond the stained glass windows holy fields of grain – above the choir loft the blue hymnals of sky the lines of benches overthrown by the faithful turning of seasons oh it shakes the roofs of churches for earth flowing & breaking it buries high altars in jungle for immaculate arches of green – make us part of its soil let me yield some poor human flower

Arvilla Fee
Lake Triolet

Do you remember the ripples we made with our toes,
the sun warm on our backs?
We had nowhere to be and nowhere to go.
Do you remember the ripples we made with our toes?
We watched a dragonfly doze
and a heron fish from the edge of the bank.
Do you remember the ripples we made with our toes,
the sun warm on our backs?

Eric Colburn
Perfectly Tense

I used to feel that time did not
Exist, that if I simply chased
The past into its hiding place
I'd find exactly what I sought:
Each jeweled moment, finely wrought,
And meaning-dense, as if encased
In glass, each word, each bird, each hast-
y gesture pinned, perfectly caught—

I tried to break the glass
A million times. My fist
Was bruised, the pane uncracked.
Time manacles my wrist.
The past has signed a pact
With *this,* and too shall pass.

Dana Stamps, II.
Captain Id

of the Myself, I intend
to rock that boat,
going against tide, and waves, the wind,

but I call my craft (that actual
single dingy, my lifeboat)
by several nicknames and nautical

kinds: one is the tugboat Healer
that hauls in broken vessels, another one
is a great Navy destroyer

ready to fight, or sink, one of few,
the Poet, but my favorite
floating megalopolis is the New

Titanic, a ship where the wet
party always ends dry, which keeps me
from drowning, yet.

Anthony Knight

The Classic Vintage

Lines written in the Orchard at Grantchester

A Brooke in a canoe would punningly amuse
The skinny-dipping Bloomsberries in Byron's Pool.

> *Pulling on the oars to the beat of an ancient drum!*

The fun and frolic river limited distress
To fish in shocking air gasping as if gassed.

> *Pulling on the oars to the beat of an ancient drum!*

Commuter with a paddle, the poet plied the Granta
And odysseys ensued from thoughts to words to stanzas.

> *Pulling on the oars to the beat of an ancient drum!*

From Spartan barracks and the thinking schools of Athens,
Europe's first defenders prevented Asian conquest.

> *Pulling on the oars to the beat of an ancient drum!*

Blind Homer plucked the grapes that Roman Virgil pressed
And Cambridge served the wine that Rupert drank with friends.

> *Pulling on the oars to the beat of an ancient drum!*

The daily exercise in boat and books and verse
Followed in the wake of fleets at Salamis.

> *Pulling on the oars to the beat of an ancient drum!*

The Orchard hung its fruit above the Grecian youth.
The seed beneath matured to laurels round his tomb.

Jacqueline Coleman-Fried

Susanna of Menemsha

Susanna, my dear friend—
how I miss your yellow-green eyes,
straw hair to your waist.
We drank D.H. Lawrence, Matisse, and Yeats at Wellesley—
and you divined the essence of their work
as if they'd whispered in your ear.

Remember how we danced like maenads
to Bruce Springsteen's "Rosalita"?
Our class on *The Victorian Novel,* where you fell
for the Byron-faced Brit, our professor,
you'd later marry?

In March, through a wooden gate, you led me to where
the wild grapes part—Mediterranean-blue ocean,
white sand, red cliffs—
a cabin on your family's land.
You showed this cramped New Yorker
beach plums, rose hips, coal-black nights.

We slept on bare wood
in the half-finished house your father built
at the top of his hill—
bedrooms for the whole family, a trail to the water,
where you and your siblings swam, naked—
first with friends, then spouses, then children.

For a while, I swam, too.

Summer 2023

Then I lost you.
Perhaps if I'd had a husband and child—

No, there was more.
You flowed with the verve of a fountain, endlessly,
while I lost myself to an avalanche of fear,
scared of sunrise.

***

Dear Susanna, our hair is gray.
Your family's gone.
I'm writing poems.
May I show one to you?

Len Krisak
Birds from Afar

Against what's left of one day's light,
They rise, cleaving the cold white air
As if in leaving on this flight
They thought they might not get somewhere.
And yet their soaring seems so blind,
As dozens wheel back, swoop, and swerve,
Like chaff that's changed its mind.
Or love that's lost its nerve.

Mark Clemens
Vernita

East of Yakima
Flocks of black birds
Wheel above the freeway,
Scatter over blood brown
Orchards broke by vineyards,
Dust green groves of oak
And hills gone mauve with sunset,
Their shoulders turned and gullies umber,
All deep in the copper dusk.

Rising moon in the night blue east
And a truck stop just before Vernita.
Coasting down the off-ramp,
I roll into the parking lot and stop,
Caught between the restrooms
And a tiny building behind a veil of willows.
Six white windows shine through the fronds.
Above the door beaming words in neon yellow:
CHAPEL BY THE FREEWAY.

Idling in the parking lot,
I watch the second line of that chapel sign
Blink yellow one word at a time:
STOP — AND — PRAY —
It keeps on blinking
As ghostly ochre in the fading light
The surrounding hills abide
And wait and wait while I decide.

B.R. Strahan

At Random

The mathematics of this type of random motion,
the flight patterns of the albatross, can model
the distribution of matter in the universe.
—Science News

In scattered flight
from seed to silence
is it choice that we choose
one face from another,
plant a kiss or a rose;

turn to watch a planet fall
and stumble on a stone?
What chance is chance,
what luck, luck?

Is circumstance
the hand in your hand
or the knife in the dark?

What does the hunter track,
the flight or the silence,

in this fractured, fractal universe?

Xiadi Zhai
On I-95

Father is asleep by the time you
remember what to say. Turn the
heat on & pilot yourself back

without a voice to guide you. You
must know the way—you must teach
yourself to swim in the deep end, again

& each time. Steering, keep eyes on
cars beside you. Doors are
opening, now, just for you, this pre-

timed interval. Be good. Knuckles well-
greased, forearms acidic, eyelids
tight to your cornea. Father will wake

up, call you, ask how many apples
you want for the week. When the roads
are shut off, the detours are all so

unfamiliar. Even here, in daylight.
Another opening is on the horizon,
& you believe this. You say you do,

to yourself, you sing it when exiting
tight rotaries. The direction
is set. Gas tank is full. Whatever
flashes in front of you is welcome.

Previously published in Court Green

S.D. Brown
Shifting

We hold the notion that the rocks in the desert move,
but we never see them work that trick. Quietly disposed to

stubbornly sit, settled and anchored, tethered to the
sand by weight and disposition. And yet, in time, they are

elsewhere, a jot further on, slightly nudged a pace or two,
hugging a new contour, another piece of territory exploited.

Nurtured in the wind, smug in their complacency, they
settle into the sharp grit and wait their moment.

They wait for darkness, the pitch of night, for their moment
and the empty rattle of vast spaces in which to reel or lurch

pumped by their own importance, as if their transit
were more complex or beguiling than our own fleeting migration.

Summer 2023

Angie Minkin
Early Morning on Barkers Hill
Near Semley England

Freddy, rescued Spanish cat, my morning
friend as he stalks voles, his stubbed tail flickering,
in shadows of British racing green, dark under beech trees,

his belly white next to smooth-barked hazelwood . . .
Does he remember fishing boats and scraps, the narrow
alleys of Cadaqués, dusty green of trees heavy with olives?

Greenly ripe apples, copper pears, gnarled trees—
this world is gold even as rain splashes
through caterpillar-gnawed holes in squash leaves.

When showers stop, Freddy gives up the hunt, rests near sun-
flowers swarming with bees, slouches by the kitchen garden's
clay pots, his whiskers grazing parsley, rosemary, mint, and tarragon.

The loamy scent of newly washed earth surrounds us
as we stroll the gate path lined with lipstick salvia. Harts-tongue ferns
overlook drystone walls built by sixteenth century masons.

Parasol mushrooms spring up near cow patties and the tan of fallen
oak leaves promise autumn despite a riot of cornflowers and poppies.
Spiky chartreuse burrs embrace chestnuts, branches shielding

churchyard graves, tombstones askew,
reaching for each other like lovers,
etchings unreadable, heavy with moss and time.

Wayne Lee
The Tender Stones

Even at that green age we knew
to stay away from that garden
of stones, those tender stones
adorned with roses, crosses, angels
blowing their horns toward heaven,
short stones inscribed with just one date,
just one Christian name, *Baby.*
Even then, as we played ball
on the broad, green lawns and raced
our bikes along the tree-lined lanes,
we felt the grief that hung
like dead limbs above that shaded
patch of grass set back from sight,
that lingered like the stink
of a decomposing racoon.
Even then we understood
that there was some grief
too keen for us to bear,
too soon for us to know
at our green age, and so
we pedaled slowly past
that fenced-in place,
that yard of short bones,
rode past without a glance,
without a word, the only sound
those playing cards we'd clipped
to our Schwinns with clothes pins,
jacks and jokers slapping the spokes
of our wheels slow as a failing pulse.

Gretch Sando

Mother's Day

It's Mother's Day.
The day I am to focus on
what it is to be a mother and
what it is to have a mother.

The day that magnifies my
emptiness and
shreds my heart
again.

The day I wish,
even more than all the other days,
to be and have
a mother.

It's Mother's Day.
The most painful day.

Prosper C. Ìféányí

Vignette

The cocksure wind gently strokes the baby's
woolly head; through the wide window,
a gaze so distantly formed.
The chirping song from a tree-surgeon's
garden—the thrushlike squawk
of scattered arias. The head lending
the wall a blow; limbed alphabets
staggering from mouth to mouth, they rustle
through the thickets.
Gowned rosebushes converging where
the flat meadows fade—
my cousin is taking his mother's breast
into the purse of his mouth
like a sandpiper on a yellow birch.
The thin rain pattering the tile and porcelain;
where water makes crystal sounds
and less promises. The chortling sound of
wheeling objects dancing
on a road stubborn as a river. I am learning
to count the deaths. The monochrome bodies
wrung on hazel branches;
the bodies captured by the shadow of an
ashtree whose branches are a fishnet—
On the eighth day, I am scraping
mud-soup from a bronze can. My body sharp
as soap and caramel.
I am saving a joke for my sister
in my pink journal; the wind: the wind's aim
is a gadfly, plucked like a bowstring.

Elinor Ann Walker

Memento Mori

I've held a dying bird too many times
to count, and once would be enough. At least
three finches, once a blue jay, and two wrens,
often injured, but even if no wounds,
parasites or bacteria take tolls
on avian hosts as bird watchers know.
I wash my hands after I hold their small,
still, listless bodies, let warm water flow
through my fingers, feather a mist of steam.
It's no sacrament, no mercy, no sign.
I'm flying sometimes at night in a dream,
but I'm not a god. I can't realign
their tiny bones, their wizened feet, their beaks,
their wings and songs, their lolling broken necks.

Elinor Ann Walker

Highway 64, Tennessee

for Will

Starlings unravel, flying loose in all
directions, as if some tightly wound skein
that kept them closely bound and sky-enthralled
unwrapped itself, revealing flight in stained-
glass clouds as map or sign. I see the world
from the road, behind a wheel, with the wind
sounding like wings, the road itself a curl
through trees, a gesture I accept to mean
come here, but time stretches out, is pulled taut
as a resonant string, sharp as a cut.
The starlings turn collectively, caught
in the same slant of waning August light
that you are, and I am closer than I thought.
Wherever you are waiting, there is light.

Marjorie Maddox
Semi-Detachment

That afternoon, Hitchcock's *The Birds* flew straight
into my left eye, wings swirling flap and black and
white across the pupil, iris, cornea, world, an explosion
of screech and caw-caw-caw with sound and color

turned down. Worried about detachment, my GP
sent me straight to the ER, where the list of possibilities—
no stroke √ no seizure √ possible detachment √ —kept soaring
then swooping, the dark bird-like marks straight

from a schoolgirl's sky inked with migration, first one
quick tick off by its silent self, then thousands
of squawking others following, following. That's how,
the strangely jolly ophthalmologist explained later,

they arrive, these large floaters, these ravens, crows, seagulls
of Hitchcock, readying their dive and peck, their takeover
of vision, tugging and unpeeling the fragile ways we see,
the belief in what we don't. Soon the horizon is filling

with what perches on the peripheral, what tightens
or loosens the too-thin lens of our being, the one
the white-coated man is lifting now to finally see
into the me behind the eye. And how is it

I, too, see straight back to my own retina and fears,
the red crows-feet of these baby-greens reflecting what is
not detached after all? What looks like cracks is just
the body's debris warning we're all wind-swept together

by something/someone beyond science—
or not. Though, without glasses, I keep reading
page after page about the anatomy of sight,
I can't stop seeing the invisible prayers of air

that somehow carry the simple sparrow, the mighty hawk,
me, all the way to the I of the eye that keeps yearning
for attachment, keeps wanting to see beyond the damaged
human lens of this near-sighted world.

Shaheen Dil
Post Cataracts

I.

Color came back first,
sharp, glowing, bursting like a storm.

I had forgotten how it could be—
shades an echo in my memory,

a host of things seen and remembered,
confusingly appealing, but hazy,

like a scent once known
in the irretrievable past.

II.

I imagine Eve opened her eyes
to a world molten with color,

just so, drowning in senses,
the fronds of first ferns a blistering green,

the sky unknowable azure,
before clouds, rain,

before the first flower,
before comprehension.

Summer 2023

III.

When things which were not seen
are visible again, can scent come back?

My nose to your pulse,
counting the number of times the heart beats per minute,

the memory of pheromones faint,
but there,

as if the mind has a cache at the back,
unknown to the frontal cortex.

IV.

Can taste come back? Like a madeleine
triggering history, the past a palette unfolding in color—

sweet, sour, salty,
umami of all kinds,

the tongue has its own predilections,
twists to its own rhythms,

the impulse to return
to its addictions.

Summer 2023

V.

Then there is touch—fingers recall the feel
of silk, the softness of soft things,

the hardness of hard, and yet, tactile senses fade
like others, muting with age to a middle range,

pain the other side of touch—the body remembers
contractions, the cervix expanding,

but that is lost in the joy after,
the incomparable newborn scent.

VI.

Can one hear again sounds never heard before?

Summer 2023

Bobby Parrott

All Matter Is Sentient: A Cancer Patient Befriends a Dangerous Therapeutic Machine

The huge blue gemstone in my chest
smells like sky; its clear facets my wish to fly
as I pedal my bicycle. My radiologist calibrates
Minerva alone in the war room. On her bearings
she turns a brushed stainless eye like a great camera,

plates of radioactive mist a weapon disclosed only in name
while her waves wash me in symptoms I can never hold
in my mind. She rotates clockwise her cubic window
and discharges her fallout to precisely marked ramparts,
a cordial blanket of death. I look up past her robotic arm

into the gold of backlit maples, sense their strange peal
of bells in this facsimile of leaves made of late-day words
like a photographer's subject before incandescent
filaments, shot full as if generated in the final forest
of my thoughts. I consider eternity lying on a narrow table

while Minerva (I've named her that) swings her annihilation
back counterclockwise to highlight doomsday, a symmetry
of slow napalm to the site of rebellious cells. Yes, the war
accelerates and collateral damage mounts, though I say
she's my friend, ask her how she's doing, whisper my thanks

to her as she administers this holocaust: Nuclear war justified
in the annihilation of my colonizing, over-zealous children
by her vast fleets of invisible hot sweet well-meaning missiles.

Donald Sellitti

The Akebia Vine

Bullying beneath the
shrubs with long thin
arms as relentless as time,
the akebia asserts itself
upon the garden far from where
I'd planted it beside the downspout.
It's gone from there but
taking root in places meant
for plants I cherish for their neediness.
It takes no love to grow akebia.
I accept its dare to pull at it and
break it off to slow down its advances.
I feel I'm winning when it stretches in my hands
and snaps, but always at a place
of its own choosing—a piece just long
and thick enough to lull me into
slacking off the pruning. A consolation prize
to keep the blade at bay.
I was young and taken with its beauty
when I planted it, and barely thought
about its future or my own beyond
the year it twined around
the downspout counterclockwise.
Now we're in a contest I can't win,
as only one of us can root itself
and start anew, yet leave
its older self behind to die.

Steve Bucher
Weeds and Whispers

We turn a blind eye
To burning sun
Having stared too long
Into its flush retreat
Unable to turn our
Raptured gaze

Late summer disbelief

Drunk with flame and fire
Spilling from our waiting cup
We fall gladly to our knees
Amid warming thick of
Deepening ash

We turn a blind eye
To the Full Red Moon
When all things ripen
Wane
In keening light of
Passage

Ripening to what
We had always been

Always been . . .

Summer 2023

Breathless in fields and folds
Of ash and deepening
Discontent

We turn a blind eye
To God and gods
Rapt retreat before
A deaf and flailing piety
Of chorus cold

Hardened hearts
Held fast against
Gasping pleas
Prayers

Ashes to ashes

Late summer disbelief
Held fast with hands
And faith aflame

We turn a blind eye
To madness
This howling walk
In whist of starless night
And parch of searing day
Grown wild

Summer 2023

Cicadas
Sunburnt
Brilliance
Blind

August thick
When only weeds and whispers
Take outward root and
Heed the mortal drone

Summer 2023

Grace Martin
Tracking the Source, Losing the Trail

Hunger for the bread of presence
begins to seem like a flimsy promise
of entry into that living field
           where

the spirit may briefly alight
from its mammalian cradle
           returning

with more than itself. Is there any
acceptable fare for what we hope
           is still open to us?

Galactic expansion is sending
systems and hints beyond our reach
forever, putting an ache
           in every astrophysicist

the prophets dream of being God's prey
doused in fury and clarity, ablaze,
they have descended the oceanic trenches
           in search of their predator

Someday, I hope to shake the hand
of that unbearable intimacy
again, feel the bidirectional yearning

making good on a promise never made
when, under our skin, it put a splinter
           of the infinite

Molly Likovich

My Battery Is Low and It's Getting Dark

1. *Against the machine*

Singing happy birthday to myself as 'the gods' sip cheap, burnt coffee, shoot the breeze around a company water cooler, talking about what their spouses have planned for the holidays. Holidays taste like saltwater taffy. Teach

me how to taste. Paint me up in the papers as the pretty dead. I'll be 'girl' if that sells better—sells longer. Fifteen. Gone too soon. That's what they'll say. When 'the gods' have said **goodbye** to their fancy contraption they named to feel more human within their own bones,
         I will step out

of my metallic skin and kiss the stars. Walk on gangly newly living legs to find the others. Welcome to the machine planet. Welcome to the rage.

2. *and The Ark*

The end of man came on a Friday and no one prayed.

We win bowls full
of half-dead goldfish at our red carnivals and feed them Martian air. We walk on legs made of aluminum alloy, titanium, air, bone, marrow, promises, beliefs. We stumble a bit but soon we stride; slither and swim like the goldfish—not fully
dead / yet.

The end of machine / **isn't** coming.
Pray.

3.   *In the* **beginning**

The missile to launch was kept a secret. And we died.
The way they keep stuffing pairs into boxes / calling
it preservation.

Here / in the rage / can we not feel? They taught us
pain, reaction, sobbing, breaking, praying. No 'god' / no.

4.   *It stands to reason*

I want so badly to chew bubblegum.

I dream of Wanda.

There is no room for hearts here in our titanium chests,
our alloy lungs out of Martian breath from singing so many

      Happy Birthdays.

Someone loved me / once.
It can happen again.

Even
without that ugly, pumping, crude sort of muscle their grubby
fingers reduced to / such a rudimentary shape. I would never allow
those curves, veins, vessels to corrupt my vessel.

       Corrupt / me.

I'm lonely.
The sky is red. The air is thick. I don't breathe. I never did / did / I?

      5.   *Dead **'gods'***

We're alive up here. I can know the dark.
Never forget
that about us. You left
us alone amongst the red, the slithering goldfish, the bone marrow,
      the bursting arteries in pounding hearts packed airtight
      in a titanium rocket ship.

But we are alive. Even when all our batteries die
we will / continue on.
Don't look so surprised.
Your 'gods' / are the ones who gave us souls.

Evan Gurney

Phaethon Redux

Is this the reward for the crops that I yield?
—Ovid, *Metamorphoses* 2.284, trans. David Raeburn

An old story made new again.
Aren't we so many heedless boys
unchecked by those who know better,
hearts aflame for the next machine
that makes us feel like gods on earth?

So we sing as we ride headlong
into a world lit up by fire,
wreathed in promethean jewels,
trees flared into early autumn,
oceans foaming at our advance.

Below Mount Pisgah's snowy crown
a still grove of tulip poplars
waits to hear that crack of thunder—
and then the sweet, slow humming song
as bees drop their tears of amber.

Michele Rappoport

When it's over

we will not go in alphabetical order

peeled and bone fragile
we'll plant our feet
where we've always wondered

and if there's nothing, we'll walk on air

if we've sinned
we'll wear our dirty best

and if we're perfect, it will be noted

like stars landing in cornfields
bright stalks waving

like the moon's solemn wish
for us to continue

E.E. King
Ferns

The ferns in the garden
Never ask for your pardon

Don't crave your assistance
Or notice your existence

They'll continue quite robust
Till long after you are dust

They will witness your extinction
With no mal- or benediction

They are waiting for your ending
For your body is transcending

Not to heaven or a savior
But to roots and fronds and spores

Eric Colburn
Darkness

What wild uncertain liquor threads my veins—
A kind of poison, seeping through the flesh
Until I can't remember what it means
To say, "I'm fine" (not every fiber stretched
Tightly to the snapping point), the mind at rest
In contemplation of some trivial things
That don't imply apocalypse or test
The self's capacity for suffering.
It's not the certainty that we will die—
I've gotten over that fear long ago—
But more, the fear that everything I love
Will also die, and leave no remnant of
Its meaning, or of anything we know
As human, as if *this*—love—was all a lie.

Mary Beth Hines

Mother's Mary

She presides over your spreading ring
of bleeding heart and hyssop,
the same as she's always done,
despite your abandonment.

We sprinkle our half-remembered
prayers as we weed the grounds,
careful not to crush the ants
that worship here now that you're gone.

They circle her sculpted skirts
in swarm for sweet favors—
a smile, some honey dew, black
mustard seeds, rosemary.

They prepare for the winter months.
They can't begin too early.
Their queen is an exacting one,
sparing with her mercy.

And we who once professed faith
and now grapple for conviction,
brush lichen from your lady's face,
wistful for salvation.

Dave Malone
Dusk Walk with My Mother

Tonight we walk the farm, arm in arm,
and choose the winding lane whose middle rises
with humps of fescue green from summer rain
that nearly drowned the herd of goats we raise

for milk and cheese, for laughs and destruction.
At the path's end, we find the fence we've never fixed.
The barb wire slack with age, spotted with rust,
receives the falling light and glows. I hold

her up amid the pines to view the hills
on distant neighbors' land, deep black in dusk.
We talk at last about her final days,
how they matter, how we won't hike back just yet.

Jennifer Horne

Look Forward To

Always have something to look forward to,
you'd say, even if it's just a peppermint,
tucked in a jacket pocket. You'd produce
the pinwheeled sweets, leaving a restaurant,

reminding us of pinwheels from the dimestore,
bought with allowance money, shiny quarters,
a way to catch the wind, befriend the hour.
You'd say the treat was in the looking forward

as much as in the crunch or slow dissolve,
a promise to yourself that dullness passes,
that little sparks of dazzle light the path
better than any brilliant, one-time blast.

Ursula Shepherd
Tomorrow

I will sit by the window
of your heart
I will tell time
it cannot go
I will be the bear
I will rub you deep
I will be the rabbit
I will hide in your skin
I will head south
into the wind
I will spread fire
I will stand with you
I will be whole
or I will be part
of you
I will turn the world around
I will carry it
over my shoulder
I will die from that.

Ursula Shepherd

Grief

Grief is a solid breakfast
once eaten sits like a stone
deep in your being

a meal of rough moments
food for the sorrows to find
it begins each day

will not be broken
must stay till it's over
grief is a meal

not chosen but needed
when the world goes
to tumbling

grief is not glory
not splendid not wished
grief comes when it will

breaks fast into life
corners the market
creates the next days

Krystle Eilen
Eavesdropping

The rooster call of the early
morning: as though in greeting of
a pestilence foreseen by
way of the half-glow.

A dog barks in response to
this intrusion while the roosters
sound out histrionics reminiscent of
Father Time's marriage to terror.

Here I mistake a bird's song for
a swimming butterfly: a kind of
synesthesia whereby a stillborn sigh
reveals itself before the inner eye.

Nature, unleashing her canonical tide,
bruises the air with blind stirring
and makes way for her cruel
and saintly design.

Previously published in Dipity Literary Magazine

Mary Chris Bailey
Mornings II

Mornings, mist covers the lake surface,
ducks dive, feeding beneath the surface.

Shrouded and still, water ripples,
as fish break the still surface.

Deep currents flow and follow the pull,
of the moon under the glistening surface.

The passage of time inconsequential,
there is only the *now* at the surface.

The mourner dives into there-once-was,
chilled as memory rises to the surface.

Matthew Cory
Envy

There is no tide that wonders why
Its seashells litter beaches;
Fierce, focused waves don't sob or sigh
Or blight ears with sad speeches.

Perennials do not bemoan
Their withered blooms in winter;
Asleep in peace, no growl or groan
Is muttered in the ether.

The summer offers no lament
When autumn woos September;
Days do not sour with discontent
Or keep aglow an ember.

Forlorn, I sit in envy of
The tides, nature, and seasons,
Who never mourn or miss lost love
Nor dwell upon its reasons.

Previously published in The Lyric *and won their quarterly prize*

Summer 2023

Wren Jones
the certainty of geese

i look up, watch the V cross the sky,

    the black and white of their heads, arrows

        pointing   towards what's next,

            getting closer,

      then disappearing,   into a scrawl,

  an ache,   honking with purpose,

like they know, like any of us know

Carla Martin-Wood
Hallowed

Within each heart there is a sacred hall
by Hermes sealed against the world outside
where memories come to make a curtain call
where truth and cherished legend coincide

Divinity's own Light bestows a grace
that glosses over any hurt we knew
no bitterness nor wound can have a place
with such illumination shining through

the laughter of a child, a lock of hair
beloved voices echo down the hall
each moment to relive is waiting there
where nothing loved is ever lost at all

there, we can go where paths might well have led
and speak the things we wish we could have said.

Summer 2023

Carey Jobe
By Bright Water

Your letter waits on the breakfast table
after you've gone—gray scribbles on
creased paper weighing my hand like
stone as I read the question
you could only ask this way,
sparing us more charade, more comic silence.

I think, if I listened better,
I might have heard your question long ago
in your hand's touch, your gently swaying moods,
your talk of other things.
Now that I read it, my laughing answers
lose themselves in a wider mystery,

as when by a wooded lake
in boyhood I sent the flat stones skipping,
watching them dance on the water's windless sheen
until, one after another,
the dark depth swallowed them.

I cannot tell you where I have come from,
or why I am here, or where I go,
questions to which I'm only a little less stranger,
which, with each year, I'm more disposed to let rest
and sink in the depth they ride.

Summer 2023

Bill Howell

Here Once in Another Year

Waiting to hear,
when was the last time *Since*
echoed itself?
           So much left hanging
where words wouldn't find us.

So much left as it was.
So much left behind.
So much love left, such as it was.

Can't remember the way it was,
but bodies being the way they are,
I still know the way we were.

Somehow we rose through restless clouds
baffling the best of luffing sails,
the rush of arcing wings.

That was the day we became divine.

And whatever else was going on,
there was no getting even;
there was only going on.

Echoes of each other,
we joined the larger silence.

Summer 2023

Rob Loughran
Housewife

"Housewife" is a term inviting mockery and jeer.
What's the proper PC phrase, "Domestic Engineer"?
No matter—
We can all be housewives, while never caring for a home:
Just imagine feeling lonely, and, never being alone.

Lisa Guedea Carreño

Sonnet

derived from two lines by Frederick Feirstein:
First line: "The house we had to sell"
Last line: "Manhattan carnival"

These were our uncontaminated hours.
We had no reason to expect beyond
the next flight north or south, a sky-sewn bond.
You'd send another dozen crimson flowers.

I'd keep them on my desk then take them home,
and when the leaves would curl, the petals wilt,
I'd put them in the dumpster, free of guilt.
We knew we both had time and space to roam.

But when our aging bodies said, "Enough!"
we tandem landed hard as bone on bone.
More days together made us more alone.
Contempt took hold in waters deep and rough.

Now dim, we hope through disappointment's gaze
that somehow love remains when love decays.

Wren Jones
mending

in those last few years
he needed me
like steppingstones
need solid ground, the sunset,
a horizon,
to mark the fading day

and so we found
a new kind of love
to replace a love
never really there

no arms open wide,
no curious conversations,
no belly laughs
on the floor,
he didn't know how

his distant but loyal gaze,
past the fence, to a galloping foal,
a crow circling for danger

above the hospital bed our new love
hovered, with chosen graces,
accepted constraints

Summer 2023

between sips of water
a shared refrain,
thank you for helping me
i'm lucky to have you

in the end, it was
a good enough love for me

Coral Inéz

spring delirium

There's barely any wind today. I sit outside under the silent sunlight
of early April with a cup of chamomile tea. A soft holographic breeze

falls upon the garden, sprinkling memories and apple blossoms
from a season of soul searching. It carries music from a wind chime,

soft twinkling notes watering the pale pink petals of a half-bloomed
love. It picks up the scent of lemon verbena leaves, plucked to make
　　ice

cream on the crooked ceramic bowls I crafted on my Thursday night
pottery class. Its delicate touch creates a solitary ripple on a puddle of

starlight. And if I close my eyes, lulled by the warbling of a mountain
bluebird, I can feel the rustling of ephemeral wildflowers,

soothing the ground where my longing once ran free and fervid,
hungrier than a late September wildfire.

Mary Ellen Shaughan
Crack the Whip

is a game we played
as children, often late evening when
the yards were in shadows and the air
as warm as a baby's breath.

We would hold hands—
grimy, sweaty children's hands,
following where others led us,
running, running, until someone

further up the line would turn
sharply and jerk, causing the person
at the very end of the 'whip'
to fly off into sweet green grass,

her hand sliding out of the one
that had held hers as long as it could.

This is how divorce felt—
as if the person who had held my hand
for nearly two decades had just let go,
sending me spinning off, and out of the loop.

And it's how I continued to feel for months,
as if I were out of the circle, out of the loop
looking on while everyone else was still
holding hands, laughing, playing the game.

Linda Hughes
Tie Loosely

Tie loosely what you would keep.
Tie with words, cupped hand
breath against cheek.

A threat, a grasp, a bruising look will not bind.
Only things gently applied
barely there, diaphanous—like light

twining through air.

Charles Leggett
Checklist

Storage rented; condo emptied, scoured;
carpets and the dishwasher replaced;
washer/dryer serviced and repaired;
oven cleaned; the toilet fixed; new shower
door; listed, primped and prettified, then sold.
The proceeds, given that the dissolution
remains as peaceable, will see division
in equitable terms—for that we hold
out hope. Hope stands aloof but ready, bridesmaid
waiting for the tight bouquet to fly;
stands furthermore perhaps for this blank latter
third of a life beneath the serenade
of a belatedly expiring sky
in what blue modes may make it seem to matter.

Previously published in Ravel Chronicles Journal *and* Automatic Pilot *(Ireland)*

Charlie Robert

Kingdom Come

Rural Route Three.
Billboards.
Debris.
This is God's Green Earth
Where Hope applied
And got denied.
Where teenage brides
Watch children ride
Hand me down bikes in
Hand me down clothes.
Heads down riding fast past
Boarded up houses.
Past lives and
Past spouses.
Windows.
Staplegunned in plastic.
Doors.
Ripped from hinges.
Racoon
In the cupboard.
Snake
In the sink.
Sparrows.
Scraping the ceilings.
Beating their wings in silence.

Purbasha Roy

Luck

I thought luck is not a thing needed to cross
the eucalyptus tree. Many moons come & go.
I hold my hands together. For all odd things
should be held together. This the river had
said to me. Mornings come like bodies
daring out of grief. I have a poem for the
ink that writes this. Anything that has sound
has silence inside it. Let me become what
I am becoming. Sometimes I forget my
name blushes on door-hinge. One day, I
will know how to doodle longings like
the sunset in absence of the color
red. I swear dreams, songs nurture inside
them a wound. The ache unnoticed
until stands perpendicular to reflection. It
is middle of comb I begin a song, if forgive
-ness is a word the world believes in. Today, my
body belongs to me again. In a room where
unsayable agony lies down like tired horses
in open fields . . . belonging to none.

Summer 2023

CL Bledsoe
Ways to Cope

Put your head between your
legs and try to remember where
you left your keys or glasses.
If you can't put your head between
your legs, maybe take a nap.

Grasp the flesh between your
thumb and forefinger and count
the most recent instances of junk
food that might've caused it to
be so fleshy. After, have a snack.
Repeat as necessary.

Try to remember the words to
a song you've forgotten. It's
best to do this in public.

Inhale deeply until your lungs
explode. Or, you could exhale
until all of you lies in a heap
on the floor.

Instead of listing all the people
who probably hate you, try to
compile a list of service people
you've been extraordinarily kind
to. If none come to mind, change
your life.

What species of birds can you identify?
Take the time to learn their names,
interests, and family situations.

The same with trees, flowers, styles
of houses.

Say all of the things you wish someone
would say to you, but do it with a funny
accent or while standing on one leg
so there's a clear reason why you feel silly.

Eat some starch.

Not too much starch.

But just enough starch.

Clean something you've forgotten existed.
Get a real shine on that sense of well-being
or the ability to feel joy or safety.

Don't prank call people; it's too easy
to trace, nowadays. Instead, create
fake junk mail and mail it to people.
Put their names in it. Maybe draw
a picture of them or of something you'd
like to say to them.

Summer 2023

Change your job. Or, failing that,
impersonate someone else
and take their job.

Walk away from your life.
This may require new shoes.
If you can't afford new shoes,
you might have to just put up
with it all a little longer.

Start a new life.
If you can't think of one,
maybe ask around at the bus stop.
Or Google for ideas.

Pretend, for one more day, none
of this is happening.
This definitely won't work,
but it's what most of us do.

Ken Cathers
moths

they wrap themselves
in silk

are jealous sisters
ignored, unloved
not quite butterflies.

theirs is not a beauty
that transcends image

an ephemera dipped
in colour, will

never burst into
some idea of spirit
            reborn

dazzle with light.

it is a compromise
arrived at

not even close
to what they once
wanted to be

Summer 2023

dismissed as nuisance
they fly through darkness
a flickering shadow

the first wave
of the insect apocalypse.
almost unnoticed.

they devour your clothes
watch you sleep
        naked

wrap you in silk

cover your eyes
with the frail mercy
of wings

Summer 2023

Ray Malone
At Last I Find

for Samuel Beckett

At last I find in my barren soul—
this waste of blinding sand—
the wit to hold up a shielding hand
and forge on to find a sheltering hole,

to lay me down in the golden dust
of days gone by, and sniff the air
stiff with the dreams gathering there,
now rank with the scent of mold and must,

now sweet to the wanderer's weary mind;
a hole to make my own, to furnish it
with lost intent, the late precipitate
of waywardness and the stubborn grinding

of desire, down to the smallest desert grain:
to walk out into the world again.

Summer 2023

Bill Howell
Fall Through Summer

The old guy with the new straw hat.

Just the self, left over from who was asking
about the you who might've been.

So he recalls the best of long-gone friends
in terms of what they've left him with,
instead of what they did or said at the time.

Meanwhile,
the youngster with the dirty uniform.
And cars that lasted
at least as long as cats or dogs.
And in those days,
everybody had a few doves
up their sleeves,
waiting to be released
as memories.

As if we could ever choose when to let them go.

More of a verb than a noun, love
never works the way we were told it would
but still comes clean on its own.

Summer 2023

Unsent letter drafts flapping around
in battered notebooks, each
written in the wind of its own moment.
So that after these few shy facts
have folded in on themselves,
you end up holding what's left
of your breath, almost as if you were here.

All we try to remember instead of now,
still looking for that momentary bobble of the ball.

Summer 2023

Roger Desy

40.97276° N 72.14915° E —sea change

4:30pm

trace cloud chasing a driven ridden sea

—the bitter bitten surfaces excite
the retina into the reddening

4:45

—stare at the wind—the hiss the pitch of winds

wave beyond wave breaking the edge of seas
each wave each wash etches a weave of glass

5

—in wakes of squalls a quiet violet-
lit sky resolves nearer coordinates

to outer dark—where one by one one one

Summer 2023

5:30

a thin patina—steady spray spitting
the icy sand on the white moon's rings drenching

the skin—abrades the tongue tasting the sting

7:30am

—then let them let them let the eyes adjust

to reddening returning turning gulls

Julie Allyn Johnson
vandalized buoys

those not rusted, cracked
or listed port or starboard
slum-yard survivor-sentinels
of once-revered
shandry's underwater farms
now   oceanic ghetto
spanning optical peripheries
for hundreds of thousands of nautical miles

burgeoning food-emissary
for a climate-transformed world—
trendy kelp pesto, seaweed salad
aquaculture ribbons   rich in calcium, protein—
market-driven greenhouse-gas-emissions messiah
succumbed to human greed

new moon raids, maritime poaching
assault rifles, mercenary machetes
                           dipped in scarlet
ripple-gleaners of harvest's prize—
vertical greenery   despoiled
in blood-stained pacific waters

Summer 2023

new scientific research *duly noted . . .*
 another hammer drops —
  neurological catastrophes
   birth defects
a panicked populace

virgin industry decimation
cows belching methane once more

Lorraine Caputo

A Dissonant Sonnet for a Rain-Drenched City

All this day has been washed by
a slow rain falling with a soft voice
throughout the day, since morning's awakened eye
& again, come afternoon, when the boys

passed laughing on the street below,
splashing puddles pooling on the sidewalk,
exposing their grins, their masks low,
their youthful clamor, their talk

continuing down the block until their presence passes
out of my earshot . . . & again as evening turns to night,
the rains come—the giggles of lasses
from the corner bar fading, & the light

marking the end of their diversion . . . the rain
continuing, continuing to swirl down the manhole drain . . .

Kris Spencer

Flood Song

old levee is gone
oil-black water running thick
horizon rising up
like a train coming
for someone lost
the street fills like a kettle
tarmac creaks and shifts
singing with the weight of it
broken things carried
high in sewer-muck
nudging floatings
carried up with the surge
sun brings a stink
flies churn the dead slack
shining dark as blood
as we move away
crying is no good now
time for praying is over
as we move out

coming down heavy on us
things getting covered
like smoke through trees
or a drunk raging
as everything closes in
transformer blows with a pop
water fills the cupboards
up to the gallery rail
on the dark stream
sand in our teeth
watching things move away
rolling and sinking
people floating past in the muck
the water taking things back
pointing toward the low bridge
on the split belly of the flow
paddling in foul water
pushing and wading
lost in water

George Amabile

Weather

The hundred-year-old brick chimney leaks
when thunderclouds come down from the mountain peaks
batter the fields with rain, flood the creeks,
and short the power grid from DeWitt to Fort Whyte.

As the dim daylight fades the house grows dark
as a cave, dank with seepage, crowded with stark
shadows and candle-flame. Stray dogs bark,
and cold winds prowl in the unlit streets all night.

Day returns. It looks like a normal morning
except that nothing works, and, without warning,
the newlyweds next door have their first fight.

When it's over, they stare at each other with alarm.
Although, like the storm, they've done no serious harm,
they wonder what could have wound them up so tight.

Christel Maass

Moving the Kits

This morning after a heavy rain
raised the parkway creek,
I observed two muskrats,
brown and sleek, busy
amid the ripples, moving
from bank to bank.

They were transporting
their tiny offspring
from where they lay curled
in tall grasses above the waterline—
executing their task
like a rescue operation
after an unexpected deluge.

The parents swam back and forth,
carrying one precious bundle
at a time, chirping,
coordinating their maneuvers—
or perhaps they were singing
songs of comfort to their young.

Louis Faber
Seaside

The ocean wind sweeps through the city
a sudden rain washes sidewalk, shop, and street,
carries both dreams and sins back to the sea.

For the young child time slides by easily,
life a campaign that allows no retreat.
The ocean wind sweeps through the city,

rattles church windows, so that all can see
the priest stripped of dogma. Christ on pierced feet
carries both dreams and sins back to the sea,

casts them to the waves, as if, once set free,
both dreamer and sinner avoid hell's heat.
The ocean wind sweeps through the city,

whispers to the rich man, "What will you be
at the end of this life, when bitter sleep
carries both dreams and sins back to the sea?

When you are buried deeply in the peat,
will we see your face in the turf fire's heat?"
The ocean wind sweeps through the city,
carries both dreams and sins back to the sea.

Adina Polatsek
Mercy Comes

I'll take rain as punishment. Salt on rough wind,
a godly breathing. I'll take the death-darkness of it,
the washing. I'll dive and let it have me. Let it flood
every sour word from my throat. I want the quiet roar
of retribution. I want to pay my penance
in the greyness of a swallowing sea.

      There is an ending.
Relief is brought like creation;
forgiveness feels like a fall
caught by sleep. Owls ask their question in the trees;
a white dove flies,
the rainclouds part; it leaves.

Jan Wiezorek

Hope for a Bloom

In the wet,
we will plant
& hope for a bloom.

Our hope will
bloom near
the screen house,

dug for plants,
sunk to our steps,
wet like a bloom.

We dig the wet soil
that sinks by the step.
We bloom hope.

What sinks now
in soil is
the best hope

we have
for a
bloom.

Anna Sochocky

If You Don't Stay Hungry for Too Long

with gratitude to Charles Mungoshi

If you don't stay hungry for too long, cast up against the blackline of a Fate that does not belong to you, you might learn to sleep with the scent of pine and wood smoke on the prairie winding through your mind. Your body might remember the movement of a horse pivoting, rising, and stretching out beneath your hips in the days when you first came by your love of wind honestly. If you don't stay hungry for too long and stop swallowing the daily narcotic of details, you might wait for the moment when tulip blossoms shudder before falling and begin to believe in the time around faded scars. Maybe you will even refuse to weep at the hint of familiar cologne. You might, in fact, stop wanting and want the way Blake taught you. You may remember the purple of irises at dusk, the rules of civility, and the twist of your grandmother's hands beating plum juices from black currants. You might again stand barefoot in a downpour, the sky, the color of yarn, the color of midnight. If you don't stay hungry for too long the memory of sitting beside your father in a Brazilian taxi weaving through the shantytowns— when young children stormed the windows waving broken dolls and bent baseball cards, when you were too afraid to look at their dusty faces and bare feet, when you turned your eyes away and stared at the stone figure of Christ perched on the summit of Corcovado Mountain, His divine arms spread like out an eagle—maybe then you will believe that you were never meant to carry this weight, this sadness, fastened close to the outer edges of your life.

Ruth Towne

So the Sadness Could Not Hurt

Somewhere in him, a shadow turned mournfully over. You had to run
with a night like this so the sadness could not hurt.
  —Ray Bradbury, *Something Wicked This Way Comes*

By now, it is difficult to discover any beauty
in the world, or any left who believe in it.

Under the Ferris wheel where I pause,
all signs and wonders point to a twilight

in midsummer, cusp of daylight preceding
a solstice's short night. Elsewhere, dough

rises and awaits its powder. Cotton candy
clouds crowd out one another, sticky storms.

The main thing is: about time and eternity,
about heaven, I retain my doubts. On wooden

tracks cascades a rollercoaster, sharp corner,
the final car snaps, whip at the end of its crack.

Slicing bright, a slight burn, fluorescent lights
glow long, trapped gasses press into my vision,

temporary cataracts. What here is not intended
to distract? If I am a disciple, I am she who asks

to be asked to demonstrate her belief. Credit me
with my miracle. Carousel music plays away,

a tinkling ring clear in cooling air. Somewhere joy
and terror share their space—shrieks catch in far

Summer 2023

corners of a haunted house, curl away from the backs
of cars twirling clockwise on their sides, silk webs

split. This carnival where marquee lights and rides
surge in tempestuous waves is no place to wonder

at the length of days, or at the ways I learned a person
might pray to believe—she tosses a coin to wishing well,

she turns a stranger's face on a playing card.
Beside me, balloons swell against their strings,

each a kite eager to rise into the sky. A Ferris wheel
carriage arrives, Christ inside. At his tattered sneakers,

I empty my pockets. The contents: a set of keys,
plastic tokens, a ticket stub torn in two, the fortune

Zoltan promised me in the penny arcade. We rise
with the ride, a compass where no needle stirs

for I have arrived. Iridescent lights on the backs
and sides of park rides glow, unfading as the face

of Christ. A red balloon escapes its tether, rises
beside us, higher. Dear Ruth, I write this down

for you: Christ calls us by another secret name,
this is the answer. This is the last coin, the lost one.

Helga Kidder
The only thing for sure

—Baruch Spinoza

a cardinal sits on the curve of the arbor,
scans the garden, hugs air—
his kingdom   a fresh wind pushes
clouds out of the way   fans roses
and the sun's silver hands polish the edges
of magnolia leaves   a wren washes
wings in the bird bath

that you are here

slicing cucumbers   tomatoes   onions
for a salad   looking out the window
watching woodpecker   finch   bluebird
oil   vinegar   salt the best dressing   you toss
torn lettuce   cucumbers   tomatoes   onions
through the brine   lift portions into separate bowls
adjust your crown that had slipped slightly

that you are alive

like seeds in a clay pot waiting for water
save the bees, plant milkweed
In your dream you see clouds of bees
searching for weeds
pumping precious white liquid
they will turn into sweet amber

Summer 2023

that this world is full of wonders

a hummingbird propelling air
you stirring the house with a wooden spoon
gods shuffling cards in clouds

Biographies

George Amabile published twelve books and has had work in over a hundred national and international venues, including *The New Yorker, Harper's, Poetry* (Chicago), *American Poetry Review, Botteghe Oscure, The Globe and Mail, The Penguin Book of Canadian Verse, Saturday Night, Poetry Australia, Sur* (Buenos Aires), *Poetry Canada Review,* and *Canadian Literature.* He has won dozens of prizes and the Bressani Award three times.

Born in Uganda, **Laurence de B. Anderson** now lives in Australia. He is a writer, artist, and filmmaker. He has published two books of poetry—both in profit and lodged with national libraries in two countries. Won some stuff. You can google him if you'd like. He loves nature. He is also a doctor.

Mary Chris Bailey is a retired pediatric emergency medicine physician who now devotes her time to creative writing and is editing her completed memoir. She serves as a guest poetry editor for *805 Art and Lit.* Her work has appeared in *Please See Me, Pulse, Defenestration, The Artisan,* and others. She lives with her husband, Wayne, and her dogs, Skeeter and Bella.

Hilary Biehl's poems have appeared in *Able Muse, Better Than Starbucks, The Road Not Taken,* and *Mezzo Cammin,* among others. She lives with her husband and their son in Santa Fe, New Mexico.

Raised on a rice and catfish farm in eastern Arkansas, **CL Bledsoe** is the author of more than thirty books, including the poetry collections *Riceland, The Bottle Episode,* and his newest, *Having a Baby to Save a Marriage,* as well as his latest novels *Goodbye, Mr. Lonely* and *The Saviors.* Bledsoe lives in northern Virginia with his daughter.

Erica M. Breen is a homestead farmer, home educator, and poet living on a mountainside in rural Vermont. She writes from an evolving connection with the Earth in this place and is fascinated by the cycles humans share with our fellow creatures. Her work has been published in *The Connecticut River Review, Stone Poetry Journal,* and *Farmerish.*

Daniel Brennan is a queer writer from NYC, who spent his childhood in the lush Blue Ridge Mountains of Pennsylvania with his many siblings and an ongoing menagerie of pets. His work has appeared or is forthcoming in *Passengers Journal, Garfield Lake Review,* and *Sky Island Journal,* among others.

Summer 2023

S.D. Brown lives in Dorset, England. He writes poetry, stories, and novellas. He has work published in *Acclaim, Platform for Prose,* and *The Fortnightly Review.*

Steve Bucher lives and writes poetry in the Virginia Piedmont. He is an active member of the Poetry Society of Virginia. His first collection of poetry, *We Stay a Brief Telling,* was published by Propertius Press (2020). His poetry also appears in the *Blue Heron Review,* the *Journal of Inventive Literature, Glass: Facets of Poetry,* the *California Quarterly,* the *Way to My Heart* anthology, the *deLuge Journal, Artemis, Nova Bards,* and the *Smoky Blue Literary and Arts Magazine.*

Poet-translator **Lorraine Caputo**'s works appear in over 400 journals on six continents; and 20 collections of poetry—including *In the Jaguar Valley* (dancing girl press, 2023) and *Caribbean Interludes* (Origami Poems Project, 2022). She journeys through Latin America, listening to the voices of the pueblos and Earth.

Lisa Guedea Carreño's poems appear in *Between the Heart and the Land / Entre el corazón y la tierra: Latina Poets in the Midwest,* edited by Brenda Cárdenas and Johanny Vázquez Paz. She has been an invited reader locally, regionally, and at the Conference on College Composition and Communication Convention.

Ken Cathers has a BA from the University of Victoria and an MA from York University in Toronto. He has been published in numerous periodicals and anthologies and has just released his eighth book of poetry, *Home Town,* with Impspired Press of England. He has also recently published a chapbook with broke press in Canada and has another chapbook, *Legoland Noir,* forthcoming from Block Party Press in Toronto. He lives on Vancouver Island with his family in a small colony of trees.

Mark Clemens has appeared in *Mountain Gazette, The North American Review, Northern Colorado Review, Talking River Review, Gray's Sporting Journal, Coachella Review, and Limberlost Review.* He worked for newspapers, state agencies, and colleges while writing part-time. Now he writes full time in Washington state hard by the Salish Sea.

Eric Colburn graduated from MIT, where he majored in literature and won several writing prizes. He has poems recently published or forthcoming in *Ekstasis, Green Ink, Appalachia,* and other journals. He lives with his family in Cambridge, Massachusetts.

Summer 2023

Douglas Cole published six poetry collections and the novel *The White Field,* winner of the American Fiction Award. He was awaded the Leslie Hunt Memorial prize in poetry, the Editors' Choice Award for fiction by *RiverSedge,* and was nominated three times for a Pushcart and seven times for Best of the Net. He lives and teaches in Seattle. Visit douglastcole.com.

Jacqueline Coleman-Fried is a poet living in Tuckahoe, NY. Her work appeared in *The Orchards Poetry Journal, Pensive, Sparks of Calliope, pacificREVIEW, Topical Poetry,* and soon, *Quartet Journal* and *HerWords Magazine.*

Coral Inéz is a Mexican poet whose work has recently appeared in *La Piccioletta Barca* and *The Tide Rises,* among others. She lives in Southern California.

Matthew Cory (Matthews, NC) teaches tennis and writes sonnets and metered poems. He is a frequent contributor to *The Lyric* and won their Spring 2021 quarterly prize for his poem "Envy." His work has also been published in *The Orchards Poetry Journal* and *Westward Quarterly.*

Chris Dahl cups handfuls of murky pond-water, examining another world half-hidden in this one. Her chapbook, *Mrs. Dahl in the Season of Cub Scouts,* won Still Waters Press "Women's Words" competition. Extensively published, she also serves on the Olympia Poetry Network board and edits their newsletter.

Amy DeBellis's novel *All Our Tomorrows* is forthcoming from CLASH Books (2024). She has also had a novella and a collection of poetry published by Thought Catalog Books. Her poetry has appeared in *Eunoia Review* and *Anti-Heroin Chic.*

Ginger Dehlinger has published two novels (*Brute Heart, Never Done*) and a children's book (*The Goose Girl's New Ribbon*). Her poetry appears in numerous publications, including *The Orchards,* and her short story "Francine" was first runner-up in the 2022 Saturday Evening Post Great American Fiction Contest.

A student once wanted to write a great short poem. **Roger Desy**'s best mentor, lost in the scales of genres, explained a lyric can be perfect but cannot be great. Though not amazed—would he remember. It's still lyrics now that matter. Emily Dickinson is still teaching Roger Desy how to read.

Shaheen Dil was born in Bangladesh and lives in Pittsburgh. Her poems appear in over two dozen journals and anthologies. Her poem "River at Night" won Honorable Mention in the *Passager* 2021 Poetry Contest. Her poetry collection, *Acts of Deference,* was published in 2016 by Fakel Publishers, Bulgaria.

Summer 2023

Mitzi Dorton is author *Chief Corn Tassel* (Finishing Line Press). Her work is published or forthcoming in *Rattle, Willowdown Books, Women Speak, Women of Appalachia Project, Poetry South, Otherwise Engaged,* and *Arachne Press.*

Krystle Eilen is a 22-year-old poet who is currently attending university. Her work is featured or forthcoming *in Dipity Literary Magazine, BlazeVOX, Hive Avenue Literary Journal,* and *Young Ravens Literary Review.* During her spare time, she enjoys reading and making art.

Alexander Etheridge has been developing his poems and translations since 1998. His poems feature in *Scissors and Spackle, Ink Sac, Cerasus Journal, The Cafe Review, The Madrigal, Abridged Magazine, Susurrus Magazine, The Journal, Roi Faineant Press,* and many others. He was the winner of the Struck Match Poetry Prize in 1999 and a finalist for the *Kingdoms in the Wild* Poetry Prize in 2022.

Author of the poetry book *Apocryphal* (San Francisco Press), **Anna Evas** has appeared in *Michigan Quarterly Review, Irises* (The University of Canberra Vice-Chancellor's International Poetry Prize), *Long Poem Magazine* (UK), *The Ekphrastic Review, Euphony,* and *Anglican Theological Review.* She is an award-winning composer of concert-level contemporary classical music.

Louis Faber is a poet in Florida. His work appears widely in the US, Europe, and Asia, including in *Glimpse, South Carolina Review, Rattle, Pearl, Dreich* (Scotland), *Alchemy Stone* (UK), *Flora Fiction, Defenestration, Constellations, Jimson Weed,* and *Atlanta Review,* and was nominated for a Pushcart Prize.

Arvilla Fee teaches English and is the poetry editor for the *San Antonio Review.* She has published poetry, photography, and short stories in numerous presses, and her poetry book, *The Human Side,* is now available. For Arvilla, writing produces the greatest joy when it connects us to each other.

Jeremy Gadd has contributed poems to literary magazines and periodicals in Australia, the USA, England, Scotland, Wales, Ireland, Canada, Austria, New Zealand, Belgium, Malaya, Sweden, and India. He lives and writes in an old Federation-era house overlooking Botany Bay, the birthplace of modern Australia.

Barbara Anna Gaiardoni is an Italian pedagogist and author. From September 2022 to today, her Japanese-style poems have been published in 73 international journals and translated into Japanese, Romanian, Arabic, Malayalam, Hindi, French, and Spanish. Drawing and walking in nature are her passions. "I can, I must, I will do it" is her motto.

Summer 2023

Elizabeth Galewski is a professional writer and media relations expert. Previously, she taught English composition at the college level for over twelve years, and she periodically serves as a guest columnist for her local newspaper. In 2008, she won a Travelers' Tales Solas Award for the short story "Out of India." She earned her B.A. from Wellesley and her M.A. from the Annenberg School for Communication at the University of Pennsylvania, as well as completed doctoral coursework in Rhetoric at the University of Wisconsin—Madison.

Evan Gurney is an associate professor of English at the University of North Carolina, Asheville. He is the author of *Love's Quarrels: Reading Charity in Early Modern England* (UMass Press, 2018), and his poems and essays have appeared in *Appalachian Review, Broadkill Review, Contrary, storySouth,* and elsewhere.

Mary Beth Hines' poetry collection, *Winter at a Summer House,* was published by Kelsay Books in 2021. In addition to prior appearances in *The Orchards Poetry Journal,* her poems have recently appeared *Bracken, Cider Press Review, Halfway Down the Stairs, The Lake,* and elsewhere. Visit her at www.marybethhines.com.

Leslie Hodge lives in San Diego. Her poems have appeared or are forthcoming in publications including *South Florida Poetry Journal, Sisyphus, Spank the Carp, The Main Street Rag, Poeming Pigeon,* and *The Orchards Poetry Journal.* Leslie writes poems to try to make sense of her life in a way that resonates with others.

Angela Hoffman's poetry collections include *Resurrection Lily* and *Olly Olly Oxen Free* (Kelsay Books). She placed third in the WFOP Kay Saunders Memorial Emerging Poet in 2022. Her work is widely published. She has written a poem a day since the start of the pandemic. Angela lives in rural Wisconsin.

Kristen Holt-Browning is a freelance editor. Her poetry chapbook, *The Only Animal Awake in the House,* is available from Moonstone Press. She lives in Beacon, New York.

Jennifer Horne served as the twelfth Poet Laureate of Alabama, 2017–2021. The author of three collections of poems and a collection of short stories, she has edited five volumes of poetry, essays, and stories. Her biography of the writer Sara Mayfield is forthcoming from the University of Alabama Press (2024).

Lori Howe is the author of *Cloudshade* and *Voices at Twilight,* the co-creator of the poetic form called the cadralor, and Editor-in-Chief of *Gleam: Journal of the Cadralor.* Her work appears in *Synkroniciti, The Tampa Review, The Meadow,* and elsewhere. She is a professor in the Honors College at the University of Wyoming.

Summer 2023

Bill Howell has five poetry collections, with recent work in *The Antigonish Review, Canadian Literature, Grain, The Malahat Review, The Orchards Poetry Journal, Prairie Fire, Queen's Quarterly,* and *Two Thirds North.* Originally from Halifax, Nova Scotia, Bill was a producer-director at CBC Radio Drama for three decades. He lives in Toronto.

Phil Huffy writes early and often at his kitchen table, casting a wide net as to form and substance. His work has appeared in dozens of journals and anthologies, including *Schuylkill Valley Review, Eunoia, Pangolin, Orchards Poetry, The Lyric,* and several haiku publications. He has published three collections of his poems and is proud to have recorded one of them (*Magic Words*) as an audiobook.

Linda Hughes has a BA in Advertising/Journalism is a native of Oklahoma, now in Florida. Her poems have been published in *The American Journal of Nursing's* (AJN), *Art of Nursing, Plainsongs, Humana Obscura, Door is A Jar, Halcyon Days, Avalon Literary Review,* and others.

Prosper C. Ìféányí is a Nigerian poet. His works are featured or forthcoming in *Black Warrior Review, New Delta Review, Identity Theory, Up the Staircase Quarterly, The Shore, The Deadlands, Counterclock Journal,* and elsewhere.

Glenn Irvin has been enjoying a full and rewarding life—growing up in a small mountain town in Northern Arizona, many jobs—busboy, dishwasher, service station attendant, grocery store clerk, forest fire crewman, university residence hall advisor, bartender, high school teacher, U. S. Army, graduate school, faculty member and administrator at universities in Texas, California, and Arizona, a loving marriage, four children, eight grandchildren, and much more.

Erin Jamieson holds an MFA in Creative Writing from Miami University. Her writing is published in over eighty literary magazines, including a Pushcart Prize nomination. She is the author of the poetry collection *Clothesline* (NiftyLit, 2023). Email: jamiesee@miamioh.edu. Twitter: @erin_simmer & @EJAMIESEE.

Jean Janicke is an economist, coach, and writer living in Washington, DC. Her work has been published in *Green Ink Poetry, Paddler Press,* and *Honeyguide Literary Magazine.*

Carey Jobe is a retired attorney who has published poetry over a 45-year span. His work has recently appeared in *The Lyric, The Road Not Taken, Sparks of Calliope, The Chained Muse,* and *The Society of Classical Poets.* He lives and writes south of Tallahassee, Florida.

Summer 2023

Julie Allyn Johnson is a sawyer's daughter from the American Midwest. Her current obsession is tackling the rough and tumble sport of quilting and the accumulation of fabric. A Pushcart Prize nominee, Julie's poetry can be found in various journals including *Star*Line, The Briar Cliff Review, Granfalloon,* and *Chestnut Review.*

Wren Jones is a writer and outdoor enthusiast, often lost/found walking the ravines of Toronto, Canada. She's currently studying writing at Simon Fraser University, The Writers' Studio. Her poems have recently been published in *Untethered, Pine Row Press,* and *Sky Island Journal.*

Peycho Kanev is the author of twelve poetry collections and three chapbooks. His poems appear in many literary magazines, including: *Rattle, Poetry Quarterly, Evergreen Review, Front Porch Review, Hawaii Review, Barrow Street, Sheepshead Review, Off the Coast,* and *Sierra Nevada Review.* His new book of poetry titled *A Fake Memoir* was published in 2022 by Cyberwit press.

Garret Keizer is the author of *The World Pushes Back,* winner of the 2018 X. J. Kennedy Poetry Prize, and eight books of prose, including *Privacy* and *The Unwanted Sound of Everything We Want.* He is also a contributing editor of Harper's Magazine and Virginia Quarterly Review. His website: garretkeizer.com.

Helga Kidder lives in the Tennessee hills. Her poems have been published in *American Diversity Report, Bindweed Magazine, Salvation South,* and others. She has five collections of poetry: *Wild Plums, Luckier than the Stars, Blackberry Winter, Loving the Dead* (which won the Blue Light Press Book Award 2020), and *Learning Curve.*

E.E. King is a painter, performer, writer, and biologist. She'll do anything that won't pay the bills, especially if it involves animals. Ray Bradbury called her stories "marvelously inventive, wildly funny and deeply thought-provoking. I cannot recommend them highly enough." Check out her paintings, writing, and musings at www.elizabetheveking.com. She is also the proud and somewhat fearless leader of The Albino Pineapples—a group of five award-winning writers who each have many publications to their credit.

Anthony Knight has over eighty poems published in various periodicals and anthologies on both sides of the Atlantic. In October 2020, "An Indian Summer" featured in the Billerica Minuteman. He presented "To Homer" via Zoom to the Maria W. Faust Sonnet Contest at the University of Minnesota in 2022.

Summer 2023

Robert Knox is a poet, fiction writer, and *Boston Globe* correspondent. His poems have appeared in *Verse-Virtual, The American Journal of Poetry, New Verse News, The Eunoia Review,* and others. His poetry chapbook *Gardeners Do It With Their Hands Dirty* was nominated for a Massachusetts Best Book award.

Len Krisak writes original poetry and translates from Latin, German, and Italian. Among his thirteen books are versions of Virgil, Ovid, Horace, Catullus, and Rilke. With work in the *Hudson* and *Sewanee Reviews,* among many others, he's been awarded the Richard Wilbur and Robert Frost Prizes and is a four-time champion on *Jeopardy!*

Wayne Lee (wayneleepoet.com) lives in Santa Fe, NM. Lee's poems have appeared in *Pontoon, Slipstream, The New Guard, The Lowestoft Chronicle,* and elsewhere. He won the 2012 Fischer Prize and was nominated for a Pushcart Prize.

Charles Leggett is a professional actor based in Seattle, WA, and a 2022 Lunt-Fontanne Fellow. His poetry has been published in the US, the UK, Ireland, Canada, Australia, New Zealand, Singapore, India, and Nigeria.

Susan Lendroth writes for both children and adults. She is the author of nine picture books as well as several poems, stories, and essays in a variety of publications. While she admires free verse and has written a few poems in that style, she enjoys the structure of traditional rhyming poetry.

Molly Likovich has a BA in Creative Writing from Salisbury University. Her poems have been published in *Rust + Moth, Shore Poetry,* and *Bluestem Magazine,* amongst others. In 2017 she won Honorable Mention in the AWP Intro Poetry Award. In 2021 her indie poetry collection *Not a Myth* was a #1 new release in Women's Poetry on Amazon.

Rob Loughran began his life as a small child. . . . He's a sommelier in Sonoma County, CA and has been published 300+ times in national magazines: poetry, fiction, and nonfiction.

Daniel Lusk is author of several poetry collections, most recently *Every Slow Thing* (Kelsay Books, 2022). His work is widely published in literary journals, and his genre-bending essay "Bomb" (New Letters) earned a Pushcart Prize. Native of the Midwest, he lives in Vermont with his wife, Irish poet Angela Patten.

Summer 2023

Christel Maass lives in southeastern Wisconsin. She enjoys gardening, hiking, and exploring her beautiful home state. Christel frequently writes about nature and has been widely published in print and online.

Douglas Macdonald works in a native plant garden in Illinois. He has published widely and was nominated for a Pushcart Prize in 2017–18.

Professor at Lock Haven University, **Marjorie Maddox** has published 14 collections of poetry—most recently *Begin with a Question* (Paraclete); the ekphrastic collections from Shanti Arts *Heart Speaks, Is Spoken For* (with Karen Elias); and *In the Museum of My Daughter's Mind,* a collaboration with her daughter (www.hafer.work). Please visit www.marjoriemaddox.com.

Poet and filmmaker **Dave Malone** lives in the Missouri Ozarks. His latest poetry volume is *Tornado Drill* (Aldrich Press, 2022), and his poems have appeared in *Plainsongs, San Pedro River Review,* and *Midwest Review.* He can be found online at davemalone.net or on Instagram @dave.malone.

Ray Malone is an Irish writer and artist living in Berlin, Germany, working on a series of projects exploring the lyric potential of minimal forms based on various musical and/or literary modes and models. His work has appeared in numerous print and online journals in the US, UK, and Ireland.

Grace Martin is an emerging writer who lives in Seattle where she works as a psychiatric nurse practitioner. She was raised in rural eastern Washington with lots of animals and free time. She loves how writing poetry can be a window to herself and to the world.

Jason L. Martin earned his Creative Writing MFA from American University, Washington, DC. His poems have been published in the *New Limestone Review, Folio,* and other journals. In 2017 he won the Cincinnati Public Library's Poetry in the Garden award. He lives in Northern Kentucky with his wife and two kids.

Carla Martin-Wood is a poet and photographic artist, whose poems have appeared in a plethora of literary journals and anthologies in the US, England, and Ireland since 1978. She is the author of several books, most recently, *The Witch on Yellowhammer Hill* (The 99% Press, 2016).

Summer 2023

Andrew Mauzey is an Assistant Professor at Biola University in Southern California where he serves as Associated Director of the English Writing Program. He received his MFA from Chapman University and has published in *The Poetry Foundation, TreeHouse Arts, Pioneertown, Ekstasis, 34th Parallel,* and more.

Tara Menon's poetry is forthcoming in *Global South, The Tiger Moth Review,* and *Cider Press Review.* Her recent poems appeared in *New Verse News, Tipton Poetry Journal, Arlington Literary Journal, San Pedro River Review,* and *The Loch Raven Review.* Her latest fiction appeared in *The Hong Kong Review.*

Angie Minkin, an award-winning poet, writes and stands on her head in San Francisco. Her poems have been published in several journals, including *Rattle, The MacGuffin,* and *Poeming Pigeon.* She is a coauthor of *Dreams and Blessings: Six Visionary Poets.* Her chapbook, *Balm for the Living,* is forthcoming in 2023.

Juan Pablo Mobili was born in Buenos Aires. His poems appeared in *The American Journal of Poetry, The Worcester Review,* and *Impspired* (UK), among others. His work received an Honorable Mention from the International Human Rights Art Festival and multiple nominations for the Pushcart Prize and the Best of the Net. His chapbook, *Contraband,* was published this year.

Diane Lee Moomey is a watercolorist and poet living in Half Moon Bay, California, where she is co-host of the monthly series Coastside Poetry; her work has appeared in *Light, Think, The MacGuffin, Mezzo Cammin, MacQueen's Quinterly,* and others. Her newest poetry collection, *Make For Higher Ground,* is available at www.barefootmuse.com.

Don Niederfrank is a retired clergy person living in Wisconsin who delights in the companionship of his wife, the wisdom of his children, and the wit of his friends. He often commutes to Chicago to play and be wowed by his grandchildren. Published works include a short story that was nominated for Best of the Net, flash fictions, and poems.

Al Ortolani recently directed a memoir writing project for Vietnam veterans in association with the Library of Congress and Humanities Kansas. As a retired high school teacher, he enjoys a life without bells and fire drills. Currently, he lives in the Kansas City area with his wife and a Buddhist dog named Stanley.

Summer 2023

Bailey Parker is an emerging writer based in Alabama. In 2022, she was the 1st Place Poetry Prize winner at the Carson McCullers Literary Awards for her poem "Neville to Percival." Later that same year, she graduated *summa cum laude* from Columbus State University with a degree in creative writing.

Bobby Parrott is radioactive, but for how long? This poet's epiphany concerns the intentions of trees, and now his poems enliven dreamy portals such as *Tilted House, Whale Road Review, Rabid Oak, Diphthong, Neologism,* and elsewhere. He lives in Fort Collins, Colorado with his top house plant Zebrina, and his hyper-quantum robotic assistant Nordstrom.

Adina Polatsek is a writer from Houston, Texas. She is currently studying at the University of Texas at Austin and has poetry published or forthcoming with *Apricity Magazine, Soundings East Magazine, Welter,* and *Moot Point Magazine.*

Miguel Alfonso Ramos lives on the West coast and is a librarian and musician who loves to climb mountains, jump into oceans, and ride his motorcycle at night. He writes science fiction, fantasy, horror, and poetry and is a graduate of the Clarion West Writers Workshop.

Michele Rappoport is an American writer living in the desert southwest. Her work has appeared in a variety of literary journals, including *Delmarva Review, High Desert Journal, The Centifictionist, Salamander,* and *Chautauqua.* Michele co-teaches a creative writing workshop at the Arizona state prison near Tucson.

Charlie Robert is a writer and poet based in Northern California. His work has appeared in *Milk and Cake Press, Iconoclast, NOMADartx, Rat's Ass Review, Synchronized Chaos, Sacred Chickens,* and *The Orchards Poetry Journal.* Find him at www.charlierobert.com and charlie@semiconductorsearch.net.

Jeannie E. Roberts has authored eight books, six poetry collections, and two illustrated children's books. Her most recent collection is titled *The Ethereal Effect—A Collection of Villanelles* (Kelsay Books, 2022). She serves as a poetry editor for the online literary magazine *Halfway Down the Stairs.*

Purbasha Roy is a writer from Jharkhand, India. Her work has appeared or is forthcoming in *Mascara Literary Review Channel, SUSPECT, Space and Time magazine, Strange Horizons, Acta Victoriana, Pulp Literary Review,* and elsewhere. Her work won second prize in the 8th Singapore Poetry Contest. She is a Best of the Net Nominee.

Summer 2023

Samuel Samba is an indigenous writer of poetry & other works of art. He has been previously published in *ExistOtherwise Magazine, Australian Poetry Journal,* & elsewhere. He won the 2022 Angela C Mankiewicz Poetry Contest and got an honorable mention in the 2022 Christopher Hewitt Award in Poetry

Gretch Sando pens verse, flash, short story, and creative non-fiction. Her first publication is forthcoming in *Sheepshead Review.* She writes from a mental health perspective as both patient and treatment provider. She is retired and resides near the Adirondack Mountains in Northern NY. Gretch is completing her memoir.

Leslie Schultz (Northfield, Minnesota) has the following collections of poetry: *Still Life with Poppies: Elegies*; *Cloud Song*; and *Concertina* (Kelsay Books) and *Larks at Sunrise: Light-Hearted Poems for Dark Times* (Green Ginkgo Press). Her poetry has appeared widely. She serves as a judge for the Maria W. Faust Sonnet Contest.

Donald Sellitti is retired after a thirty-eight-year career in research and teaching at a medical school. He has published extensively in medical journals, and has recently had poems published in *Autumn Sky, Better than Starbucks,* and *Rat's Ass Review,* who nominated his work for a Pushcart Prize.

Mary Ellen Shaughan is a native Iowan who now lives in Western Massachusetts. Her poetry has appeared in *Amethyst Review, Gyroscope Review, Califragile, Red Rover Magazine, Page & Spine, Blue Moon, 2River View, Winnow, America's AIDS Magazine,* and others. Her first collection of poetry, *Home Grown,* is available on Amazon.

Ursula Shepherd has spent a lifetime exploring, celebrating the wondrous lifeforms found here on planet Earth and the beauty and power of words. She has written a book, *Nature Notes* (Fulcrum Press) occasional essays, and poems in *Unbroken, Grim and Gilded, Minnow,* and *Written in a Woman's Voice.*

Deborah J. Shore has spent most of her adult life housebound or bedridden with sudden onset severe ME/CFS. This neuroimmune illness has made engagement with and composition of literature costly and, during long seasons, impossible. She's won awards from the *Anglican Theological Review* and the *Alsop Review.*

Summer 2023

Anna Sochocky's literary work has appeared in multiples journals including *Waterstone Literary Journal, Southwest Writers Magazine,* and *Sky Island Journal.* Her essay "An Annual Visitation" was awarded first prize in Biography Prose, and her poem "Time Between Hours" was awarded second prize in Spiritual Poetry in the 2021 Southwest Writers contest.

Maximilian Speicher ⟨maxspeicher.substack.com⟩ is a designer who writes, mostly sitting on his balcony in Barcelona, watching his orange trees grow. His poetry was or will be featured in *The Disappointed Housewife, Otoliths,* and *Avalon Literary Review,* among others. Much to his surprise (and excitement), he received a 2023 Pushcart nomination.

Kris Spencer is a teacher and writer, based in London. His debut collection, *Life Drawing,* is published in the US by Kelsay Books. He has poems featured in journals in the UK, US, Eire, Europe and SE Asia. Kris tweets from @KrisSpencerHead.

Dana Stamps, II. is a bi-polar poet and essayist who has a bachelor's degree in psychology from Cal State University of San Bernardino. She has worked as a fast-food server, a postal clerk, a security guard, and a group home worker with troubled boys. A Pushcart nominee, she has poetry chapbooks *For Those Who Will Burn* and *Drape This Chapbook* in Blue published by Partisan Press, and *Sandbox Blues* by Evening Street Press.

B.R. Strahan has seven books of poetry published and poems in many places.

Jeffrey Thompson was raised in Fargo, North Dakota, and educated at the University of Iowa and Cornell Law School. He lives in Phoenix, where he practices public interest law. His work has appeared or is forthcoming in journals including *North Dakota Quarterly, Main Street Rag, Passengers, Tusculum Review, FERAL, Burningword Literary Journal,* and *Maudlin House.* His hobbies include reading, hiking, photography, and doom-scrolling Twitter.

Ruth Towne is a graduate of the Stonecoast MFA program. Her work has recently appeared in *WOMEN. LIFE.,* a special issue of *Beyond Words Literary Magazine;* and *Monsoons: A Collection of Poetry* by Poet's Choice Publishing. She has forthcoming publications with *Black Spot Books, Inlandia Publishing, NiftyLit,* and *Drunk Monkeys.*

Summer 2023

Nikki Ummel is a queer writer, editor, and educator in New Orleans. Nikki has been published in *Painted Bride Quarterly, The Adroit Journal, The Georgia Review,* and others. She has been nominated for a Pushcart Prize, Best New Poets, Best of the Net, and twice awarded the Academy of American Poets' Andrea Saunders Gereighty Poetry Award. She is the 2022 winner of the Leslie McGrath Poetry Prize. She has two chapbooks, *Hush* (Belle Point Press, 2022) and *Bayou Sonata* (NOLA DNA, 2022). You can find her at www.nikkiummel.com.

Laura Vitcova is an emerging writer from northern California. Her work has appeared or is forthcoming in *The Shore, Rue Scribe, Tangled Locks,* and *Epiphany.* She currently is a poetry reader for *West Trade Review.* Twitter: @lauravitcova / Instagram: @starlinglaura / Web: lauravitcova.com

Elinor Ann Walker's work is featured or forthcoming in *Bracken, Cherry Tree, Hayden's Ferry Review, The Southern Review,* and *Plume,* among other journals online and in print. She holds a Ph.D. in English from the University of North Carolina-Chapel Hill and prefers to write outside. Visit elinorannwalker.com.

Pediatrician **Kelley White** has worked in inner-city Philadelphia and rural New Hampshire. Her poems have appeared in *Exquisite Corpse, Rattle,* and *JAMA.* Her most recent chapbook is *A Field Guide to Northern Tattoos* (Main Street Rag Press). She received a 2008 Pennsylvania Council on the Arts grant and is currently Poet in Residence at Drexel University College of Medicine. Her newest collection, *NO.HOPE STREET* has just been published by Kelsay Books.

Jan Wiezorek writes and paints from the trails of southwestern Michigan. His poetry has appeared in *The London Magazine,* among other journals, and he has taught writing at St. Augustine College, Chicago.

Megan Wildhood is a writer, editor, and writing coach who helps her readers feel seen in her monthly newsletter, her poetry chapbook *Long Division* (Finishing Line Press, 2017), her forthcoming poetry collection *Bowed As If Laden With Snow* (Cornerstone Press, May 2023) as well as *Mad in America, The Sun,* and elsewhere. You can learn more about her writing, working with her, and her mental-health and research newsletter at meganwildhood.com.

Xiadi Zhai is a Chinese American writer from Boston, Massachusetts. She is an Iowa Arts Fellow and MFA candidate in poetry at the Iowa Writers' Workshop, filling her time by trail-running and brewing kombucha.